SEVEN
PRAYERS
THAT CAN CHANGE YOUR
LIFE

SEVEN
PRAYERS
THAT CAN CHANGE YOUR
LIFE

HOW TO USE JEWISH SPIRITUAL WISDOM TO ENHANCE YOUR HEALTH, RELATIONSHIPS, AND DAILY EFFECTIVENESS

Leonard Felder, Ph.D.

**Andrews McMeel
Publishing**

Kansas City

Seven Prayers That Can Change Your Life: How to Use Jewish Spiritual Wisdom to Enhance Your Health, Relationships, and Daily Effectiveness copyright © 2001 by Leonard Felder, Ph.D. All rights reserved. Printed in the United States of America. No part of this book may be used or reproduced in any manner whatsoever without written permission except in the case of reprints in the context of reviews. For information, write Andrews McMeel Publishing, an Andrews McMeel Universal company, 4520 Main Street, Kansas City, Missouri 64111.

01 02 03 04 05 RDC 10 9 8 7 6 5 4 3 2 1

Library of Congress Cataloging-in-Publication Data

Felder, Leonard.
    Seven prayers that can change your life : how to use Jewish spiritual wisdom to enhance your health, relationships, and daily effectiveness / Leonard Felder.
        p.   cm.
    Includes bibliographical references and index.
    ISBN 0-7407-1895-9
    1. Prayer—Judaism. 2. Spiritual life—Judaism. 3. Inter-personal relations—Religious aspects—Judaism. I. Title
BM669.F45   2001
296.4'5—dc21

                                                                2001022272

BOOK DESIGN AND COMPOSITION BY KELLY & COMPANY

This book is dedicated to all the men and women in adult Jewish education, who give their time and talents to teach, administer, raise money, commute, study, and learn.

You have no idea how many lives are touched and improved by your efforts to spread the wealth of Jewish spiritual wisdom. Thank you for being a blessing in my life and for assisting so many other people who were hungry to learn.

Contents

Acknowledgments

Over the years many caring and wise teachers have contributed their insights to what became the book you are about to read. I am grateful to each of them for sharing their passion and their intelligence, especially Dr. Viktor Frankl, Professor Rowland Shepard, and a host of beloved rabbis, including Ted Falcon, Mordecai Finley, David Cooper, Debra Orenstein, Zalman Schachter-Shalomi, Jonathan Omer-Man, Amy Eilberg, David Wolpe, Allen Freehling, Michael Ozair, Sue Levi Elwell, Laura Geller, Abner Weiss, Harold Schulweis, Ernst Conrad, and M. Robert Syme.

In addition, several friends and colleagues, including Miriam Raviv, Anita Siegman, Ellen Winer, Michael Stroud, Deborah Bronner, Lucky Altman, Mitch Golant, Nancy Shapiro Pikelny, Monty Turner, Trudi Alexy, Peter Reiss, Teri Bernstein, as well as the staff members of the libraries of UCLA Biomedical Research, the University of Judaism, and Sinai Temple, especially Joel Tuchman, gave valuable ideas and support to this project.

My close friend, Rabbi Marc Sirinsky, a truly generous soul, found time in his busy schedule to critique each chapter and suggest books for additional guidance. Everyone should have such a good friend who can be so honest.

I am fortunate to have found an extremely knowledgeable and caring literary agent, Andrew Stuart, and a highly supportive and wise editor, Mindy Schultz, who have been enormously helpful with editorial suggestions and strong encouragement.

I want to offer my thanks to each of my family members who shared their support and love. They include Martin and Ena Felder; Janice, Craig, and Erica Ruff; Helen Rothenberg, Eddie Rothenberg; William Schorin, Jeff Schorin, June Schorin; and Ruth Wilstein.

I am extremely grateful to my wife and best friend, Linda Schorin, for her enthusiasm, insights, and love on this project, as well as her terrific support during our twenty-one years together, and I want to thank my son, Steven Alon Schorin Felder, for his excellent questions about Jewish spirituality and his curiosity about life in general, both of which I hope will continue for a long time.

Finally, I want to thank the Eternal One, the mysterious creative Source, who I believe gives us glimpses of the projects we ought to do and who helps us overcome our fears and hesitations so we can bring to fruition some of our souls' desires. I am very appreciative for all the opportunities I've been given.

Pronunciation Key

In this book you will see several Hebrew words and phrases transliterated (phonetically spelled in English letters so they can be understood by anyone who doesn't speak Hebrew). In most cases the best way of sounding out these words will be obvious to you. But there are a few letter sounds and combinations that need explanation:

When you see *kh,* think of the throaty, guttural sound in *khutzpah* (nerve or assertiveness) or *khallah* (the special bread for the Sabbath).

When you see *ei,* think of the long *a* sound in the English word *reign* or the Hebrew word *Eloheinu* (our God).

When you see *ai,* think of the long *eye* sound in the word *Thailand* or in the Hebrew word *L-khai-yim* (to life).

SEVEN
PRAYERS
THAT CAN CHANGE YOUR
LIFE

Introduction

For many centuries people have wondered, "Does prayer help? Does it make a difference in the quality of your life if you engage in quiet moments of heartfelt prayer to help resolve the dilemmas of daily living?"

Approximately twenty years ago, when I was first starting out as a psychotherapist, a highly creative and intelligent patient named Eleanor* asked me during one of our sessions, "Do you think it would help if I began to say a prayer each day about my strained relationship with my mother?"

For a moment, I pictured Sigmund Freud, the founder of one-on-one psychotherapy, *plotzing* in his grave. (*Plotzing* is a Yiddish word that means he was so uncomfortable he felt like bursting.) According to several biographers, Freud longed to be accepted by the atheistic scholars of his beloved Vienna and he was somewhat ambivalent about his Jewish roots. I believe Freud would have puffed on his famous cigar and grumbled in his thick accent, "No Fraulein, prayer is not going to help regarding your mother."

It's been almost a hundred years since Freud wrote a scathing book about faith, entitled *The Future of an Illusion,*

---

*In this book, client names and details have been changed to protect confidentiality.

in which he theorized that spirituality is a neurotic waste of time and insisted that prayer was useless in counseling.

But maybe Freud was wrong.

I told Eleanor I'd be very interested in working with her to find a prayer that could help her deal more effectively with her extremely critical and demanding mother. Over the next several weeks, we began to explore how to use prayer, meditation, and guided imagery to make each interaction with Eleanor's mom far more healthy and positive.

A few months later, on the day she completed her therapy, Eleanor said, "I can't prove for sure there's a God or that God wants to get involved with my stuff about my mother. But I've found that by praying about this issue each day—by taking a few minutes to connect with a strong, centered, and holy place deep inside my heart—I'm a lot more patient and creative with my mom and with nearly everything else I deal with these days."

Eleanor concluded, "Saying a prayer hasn't changed who my mother is: She was five-foot-one and pushy when I first started praying, and she's still five-foot-one and pushy. But these prayers have made me a lot more successful in finding my strength and my peace of mind no matter what my mother says or does."

A Growing Trend

During the past two decades, an increasing number of physicians and psychotherapists have begun to use spiritually based methods to help men and women gain access to their deeper selves as part of the healing process. Based on the research of Herbert Benson and Joan Borysenko at Harvard, Larry Dossey at the University of Texas-Dallas, Jon Kabat-Zinn at the University of Massachusetts, and Bernie Siegel at Yale, experts in mind-body healing have shown repeatedly that spiritual approaches like prayer and meditation can be an important addition to conventional methods of treatment for many physical and emotional difficulties.

Since 1980 there have been more than two hundred scientific studies on the usefulness of prayer for improving one's physical health, emotional well-being, and sense of personal effectiveness. (For a summary of the key scientific findings, see *Appendix A: Recent Research Findings About Prayer* at the back of this book). Most of these studies confirm that prayer is a subtle but powerful tool for helping a person become more connected to what matters most in his or her life. Repeated evidence from numerous research studies indicate that deeply felt prayers not only can help you feel strong and more focused inside, but they can also improve how you deal with difficult people and situations in your daily life.

As a psychologist with a lifelong interest in spiritual concerns, I wanted to see for myself whether or not prayer and meditation could help the people who came to my office for treatment. So for nearly twenty years I have been researching directly with my patients how certain prayers can assist us in our daily lives and personal struggles. I have observed many of my patients achieve remarkable results.

Keeping in mind that there are no guarantees of the effectiveness of any particular prayer in a given situation, here are some of the frequent outcomes I have witnessed from asking many of my patients to use specific prayers and guided meditations in their private lives and worldly endeavors:

- Numerous people have dramatically improved their immune systems and their ability to cope with serious illness.

- Many couples have deepened their level of intimacy and communication.

- A large number of clients enhanced their creativity by using prayers to ask for guidance and direction.

- Numerous men and women saw their concentration, persistence, and ability to overcome procrastination improve when they began using specific prayers for staying focused and on track each day.

- People have become less impatient and judgmental with themselves and their family members.

- Numerous men and women have deepened their connection to their inner voice and their intuition.

- A large number of men and women have found a deeper sense of purpose and meaning in life.

- A wide variety of individuals who were turned off by the image of God presented in childhood by their parents or religious schools found they could explore more adult and complex ideas about God through the use of the translations and interpretations presented in this book.

- Many people who often felt they were mouthing empty words of prayer deepened their connection to their spirituality through the techniques described in this book.

I urge you not to assume that these positive results will occur for you automatically after reciting a few special words. When engaging in spiritual activities such as prayer or meditation, there is no way to control how things will turn out. We can use prayer to open up to the previously untapped potential of our higher selves or to God's will, but we can't force any particular result to occur. Prayer is not about imposing your will or your ego on a situation. Rather it's about going deeply inside and connecting with a source of profound energy and support that is hard to describe or measure.

Over the years I have seen hundreds of women and men who used the prayers and meditations contained in this book attain excellent results, but I have also observed many instances in which nothing much appears to happen. Quite often the result of a particular prayer is subtle, barely visible, or not exactly what the person had intended. Prayer is a mysterious process, yet in many cases it can dramatically change your life for the better, especially in the way it can shift your nervous system away from agitation and toward greater clarity and effectiveness.

Choosing Which Prayers to Explore

Seven Prayers That Can Change Your Life offers easy-to-use translations and discussions of a select group of remarkable prayers that have been part of the Jewish liturgy for centuries, and which possess extraordinary power. Each chapter explores how to reach deeper levels of understanding of these sacred phrases and how to gain access to their mystical and healing qualities.

The prayers that have helped many of my patients are neither hard-to-learn nor do they require an extensive education in spiritual or religious topics. You don't need to know Hebrew and it doesn't matter whether you consider yourself a highly devout person, a somewhat observant person, or someone who feels quite removed from organized religion.

While there are numerous profound prayers and ideas offered in the many spiritual traditions of the world, in this book I've chosen to focus specifically on some extremely useful Jewish prayers for three reasons:

1. Prayers and teachings that originate in the ancient spiritual language of Hebrew resonate with a poetry and holiness that is deeply moving. Not only is it beautiful to hear the rhythmic sounds, but many of the words and phrases come from the teachings of the Bible, the wisdom of the prophets and sages, and the heroic story of a people who rose out of enslavement and persecution to become a moral beacon of light to the world. Learning how to express your deepest spiritual feelings in Hebrew, and to understand fully what you're saying, can be very inspiring.

2. The second reason why I'm focusing on Jewish prayers is because of the highly insightful and practical nature of

Jewish prayers and spiritual teachings. Most people, including many Jews, don't realize just how useful and profound many of these prayers are for helping men and women deal with the ups and downs of daily living. For example, in later chapters you will learn about Jewish prayers and techniques for helping you overcome procrastination, to connect with your deepest sense of purpose each day, and guide your dreams and soulful energies as you go to sleep at night. You will be surprised at how these ancient words have enormous relevance to the issues you are facing in your personal life and your spirituality.

3. In addition, there is an enormous renewed interest in Jewish spirituality and prayer right now in many parts of the world. Not only are many assimilated and nonreligious Jews beginning to study Jewish teachings, but many non-Jews are starting to explore Jewish ideas as part of their own spiritual growth. In major cities throughout the world, lectures in Kabbalah ("received wisdom teachings") and introduction to Judaism courses are filled with observant Jews, nonobservant Jews, open-minded Christians, Jungian and Transpersonal therapists, New Age seekers, and students of Buddhism and Taoism.

I grew up in the 1950s and 1960s as the child of a Holocaust survivor, and I assumed that Jewish religious ideas were scorned by the vast majority of people. But in more recent times, I've participated in dozens of interfaith dialogues between Jews and Christians, second-generation Jews and second-generation Germans, Jews and Muslims, Jews and African-Americans, and Jews and Asian-Americans. I've been impressed by how many diverse peoples are now curious about Jewish spiritual traditions and are involved in studying Jewish topics.

Millions of non-Jews are reading books about Judaism such as *The Gifts of the Jews* by Thomas Cahill, *How Good Do We Have to Be* by Harold Kushner, *To Begin Again* by Naomi Levy, *Making Loss Matter* by David Wolpe, and *Small Miracles* by Judith Leventhal and Yitta Halberstam. This is an unusual moment in history, when people of various beliefs can study and learn from each other like never before.

Who Can Benefit?

Seven Prayers is intended for readers from all levels of spiritual involvement and affiliation. To see how you might benefit from reading and applying some or all of the chapters in this book, consider which of the following descriptions sound like you or someone you know:

1. Have you recited certain prayers for years and often wondered what they really mean, where they come from, or how they actually work?

2. Have you found some prayers confusing, uncomfortable, or upsetting because you disagree with what they seem to be saying?

3. Is there a problem in your life right now that you would like to pray about, but you're not sure what words to use or how to be most effective?

4. Do you long for a deeper connection with your spiritual side or with God, but you haven't been able to find sufficient time or the right words to open up as fully as you'd like?

5. Are you looking for ways to use prayer to become a better person or to assist in the healing or recovery of yourself or someone you care about?

6. Do you have a rich inner life but want to go even deeper into the realms of prayer or meditation?

7. Are you a parent, grandparent, teacher, or concerned person who wants to make sure the next generation receives a more inspiring introduction to prayer and spirituality than you did?

A Personal Journey

When it comes to sitting down and thinking about prayer, each of us has our own likes and dislikes. For many people, it's not easy to pray. Not only does it require breaking away from the rat race of their daily lives for at least a few moments, but many people have felt skeptical or uncertain about whether prayer makes a difference and whether there is a God who listens and cares.

In my own life there are prayers that have felt empty and prayers that bring tears to my eyes each time I say them. There are prayers I didn't understand fully and prayers that speak to the depths of my soul.

I don't remember anyone teaching me exactly how to pray when I was a child. Like most curious kids, I discovered in private a way to reach out to God and ask for help. Late at night in the dark, I would listen to the silence and wonder, "Is anything there? Can something be listening to my silent words? Is there a loving presence that cares or that I can ask for assistance?"

While growing up in Detroit I learned to recite numerous prayers during many years of three-times-a-week Hebrew school. We used to have races to see who could say these ancient prayers the fastest. Several of us competed at memorizing the prayers and saying them without looking at the prayer books. But the words didn't mean much to any of us.

When I'd sit next to my beloved grandfather at his traditional synagogue I watched the observant congregants racing through the prayers so fast I couldn't keep up. I sensed there was something holy and important going on for a good number of these older men wrapped in their prayer shawls, but I wasn't sure how to partake in their intense murmuring. I felt like an outsider, and my groaning stomach made me ask God silently, "When is it going to be Ein Keloheinu or Adon Olam (the concluding songs that meant food was coming soon)?"

Even at my family's progressive temple where most of the prayers were recited in understandable English, I didn't have much connection to the deeper meaning or the profound energies of the words. They were just phrases we uttered in unison or in polite, controlled responsive readings. Sometimes a melody would move me, but the words rarely touched my heart. I wondered if they ever would.

Starting at age ten, I prayed a lot because my mother was diagnosed with breast cancer that spread to her lymph glands. Every night I asked God to keep her alive. As her cancer spread to her bones, her internal organs, and eventually to her lungs, my prayers grew more desperate. I was fourteen when my mother died. She was forty-six. I felt angry with God for not stopping the cancer, and even though I continued my Jewish studies, I wasn't sure if I would ever pray again.

Not until many years later did I begin to find teachers, books, workshops, congregations, and retreats where the words of the prayers slowly came alive. Over the past twenty years, I have been extremely fortunate to have studied with many sincere and knowledgeable men and women from all branches of Judaism who shared their insights into the secret levels of meaning that are contained in Jewish prayers and meditative practices. Both when I lived in New York and when I moved to Los Angeles, I found that there are almost no boundaries anymore in Judaism when it comes to studying and learning. I felt welcomed and guided in my adult education by numerous rabbis and teachers from Reform, Conservative, Reconstructionist, Renewal, Hasidic, and Modern Orthodox congregations.

These scholars and teachers not only helped me understand the surface layers of what the prayers mean and why we say them, but they also went much deeper to some of the subtle and mystical layers of how the prayers can affect our souls and how the act of praying can impact levels of reality that our eyes can't always see. Many different individuals helped me discover how these prayers can assist those of my counseling clients who are looking for spiritual approaches. They also taught me to look at each prayer as a mysterious work of sacred art, which the more you understand the more you can appreciate and use.

I decided to write this book because there is so much practical wisdom and healing potential to be found in certain prayers. There are profound levels of meaning that even most observant individuals haven't been taught. It's sad that most people live their whole lives with no clue about the spiritual gifts that are available. But if you find the right teachers and books that can guide you into this hidden world, a rich treasury of sacred wisdom can become part of your life and part of your family's life.

A Few Words About "God"

Since this book is about prayer, it raises the very personal issue of what you believe or don't believe about "God." I have found in my research and psychotherapy practice that each individual I interview or counsel has a slightly different point of view about what the word "God" means. One of the great strengths of Jewish spirituality is that it allows for many diverse ways of connecting with a mysterious Source that is beyond any limiting description we might think is the complete answer.

My goal in this book is *not* to tell you what you should or should not believe about the mystery of creation and how God might function in our daily lives. Instead, my goal is to describe and offer you several choices from respected Jewish spiritual teachings about how prayer can open us up to a sense of holiness, and how it can give us an experience of oneness with a mysterious soulful Presence that goes far deeper than the mundane or visible world.

I need to tell you up front, however, that when I use the word "God" or "Divine Presence" in this book, *it does not just refer to the "father up in heaven"* that you may have been taught to believe (or that you may have rejected) as a child. In each chapter of this book, I will explore with you several additional Jewish teachings on how to experience energies of support, wisdom, and strength that you may be able to access from a mysterious Source.

For example, in upcoming chapters we will be looking at how prayer can expand your ability to tap into an inner wisdom that is referred to in the Torah (the Hebrew Bible) as "the still small voice within." For many Jews, prayer is not just a calling out to the creative Source of the universe but also a way of awakening the divine sparks that we carry inside our souls.

We will also be exploring the Jewish concept of the Shekhinah (an accessible, in-dwelling Presence that some Jewish scholars refer to as an energy flow within us and between us, while others see the Shekhinah expressed in our desires for justice, connection, and caring). We will be discussing how to use prayer to open up your heart and mind to flows of energy that Jewish mystics would refer to as "divine emanations" or "shards of holy light." Finally, we will be exploring some of the Jewish teachings about how the beauty of creation and our compassionate actions to repair this broken world are among the ways we experience the energies of God.

It might be that at several points in this book you probably will say to yourself or to someone with whom you talk about spiritual ideas, "How come no one taught us these concepts when we were growing up?" The mystical and deeply spiritual interpretations of how the Infinite One expresses in our daily lives is somewhat different from the pediatric or child-oriented version that most of us were taught as children.

Once again, I urge you to read these diverse interpretations and ideas about God to stir up your own concepts and experiences. My goal is *not* to convert you to any particular set of beliefs, but only to give you a fuller understanding of the wide range of Jewish spiritual insights into the ultimate mysteries of life.

How to Use This Book

There are a few different ways to read these seven chapters and to benefit from their stories, translations, and suggestions. If you decide to read the book from cover to cover, you will gain a wealth of information about Jewish prayer and Jewish spiritual wisdom—where it comes from and how it addresses the problems, joys, desires, and special moments of daily living.

Or you might decide to read only those chapters of the book that address the specific types of prayers you find most useful. Maybe your goal is to concentrate only on prayers that can help you overcome distractibility so you can focus each day on what's most important in your life. Or maybe your longing is to explore only those prayers that deepen your connection to God. Or possibly you want to learn how prayer can improve your health or your sense of inner peace. Specific chapters address each of these concerns. You might want to stick with those particular prayers and discussions until you are ready to move on to another topic.

You might also want to use this text as a spiritual guidebook for a few weeks or months, either alone or with a family member or friend as your study partner. Look at a few pages a day or a chapter each week. Then explore what memories, feelings, and questions arise for you. Many people will find that by talking about prayer with a family member, friend, or study partner, or writing about it in a journal, they can deepen their sense of spirituality and stimulate important personal breakthroughs.

Another option is to use this book as a way to connect with other people who are also exploring spiritual concerns— as part of a class or discussion group on what it means to pray or what it means to be a spiritual human being. You and your classmates or discussion group members might want to pick one prayer each session to study or practice for a week or a month. Then see what reactions, insights, or concerns arise.

Finally, you do not have to choose the prayers in the order given in this book. Select those that call out to you—either because they are immediately the most comforting prayers or the most troubling/confusing prayers for you. Getting a strong positive or negative reaction to a prayer is one of the first clues indicating that you need to study a prayer or practice it in depth.

If the prayer immediately nourishes you, satisfies you, or brings tears to your eyes, you know it's an important blessing to which you will want to devote some time and attention in order to understand and utilize it. If a prayer offends you, upsets you, or sticks in your mind as a problem, that's another clue you have hit upon a prayer that requires additional time and study. In both cases, your spiritual life will be enhanced by your deeper understanding of the sacred words that affect you so strongly.

My goal in writing this book is to open up a passageway into the beauty and healing potential of certain prayers that have been overlooked or taken for granted for far too long. I wish someone had given me a book like this many years ago so that I could have used it to deepen my own spiritual life and to help friends, relatives, and patients who were searching for ways to connect to their own spirituality.

My hope is that you and the people you care about will use these prayers and teachings for good purposes to create healing and repair in your own lives and in the world around you. These prayers are a gift that you and I can learn to use more fully. I hope they will bring many blessings to you and the people you love.

CHAPTER ONE

A Prayer to Help You Start Each Morning with a Much Better Frame of Mind

Modeh ani (men)	I am so thankful
Modah ani (women)	
l'fanekha	in front of You,
melekh khai v'kayam	Ruling Force of life and existence,
she'hekhe-zarta be nishmatee b'khemla	Who restores and renews my soul with compassion.
rabbah emunatekha.	You are dependable beyond measure.

At six A.M. on an oldies station, the youthful 1970s voice of Carole King (born Carole Klein in New York City) floats out of my clock-radio and creeps into the auditory passages of my sleeping brain. She sings, "My life has been a tapestry of rich and royal hue . . ." These lyrics, about appreciating the underlying weave of connectedness in a hectic life, nudge me out of a dream. It's time to wake up. But my eyes are still closed, and my body pleads for another half hour of sleep. I hear the song continue as it describes our time on Earth as "a tapestry to feel and see, impossible to hold."

I love music and the memories it can stir up. But I need to get going and start the day. I switch off the radio. For a moment there is silence in the bedroom as my eyes slowly begin to let in a few rays of early morning light.

In Judaism, there are teachings that say how you deal with this half-awake moment can have an enormous impact on how your day will feel and how it will turn out. There is a traditional prayer recited first thing in the morning, when your eyes are not yet fully open and your consciousness hovers between the unseen and the visible worlds. This prayer of only twelve words can open your heart and mind to a day of profound clarity and purpose. If you understand its deeper meaning, this prayer can be a powerful tool toward a life of greater spiritual connection.

The prayer is called "Modeh" for men and "Modah" for women. It essentially lifts your mind from grumpy sleepiness or anxious thoughts about the details of the day ahead of you. These twelve Hebrew words of prayer give you a moment to connect to your deeper reality—your soul—and to feel gratitude that there is a mysterious and infinite source of compassion that dependably restores and renews your soul each day.

To understand and utilize this prayer with honesty and depth, you will first need to resolve three questions:

1. When your alarm clock jolts you awake in the morning, do you feel genuinely grateful or painfully tired—in other words, how do you want to start your day?

2. What do you believe it means to have a soul and to respond to the needs of your soul?

3. When this prayer talks of God's dependability, does it make you wonder about unanswered prayers?

By exploring these three questions, you will gain a much richer connection to the "Modeh/Modah ani" prayer and to your inner life as a spiritual human being.

Question 1
How Do You Want to Start Your Day?

If you surveyed a thousand people you might find that for at least 98 percent the first words in the morning are not *"Modeh ani/Modah ani*—I am so thankful," but rather, "Oh shoot," "Turn that stupid thing off," or "Do I have to get up?" For most people the first rush of energy the mind sends down through the nerve passageways into the heart, stomach, hands, and legs consists of a negative, grumpy feeling of resistance. The sluggish body-mind begs, "Let me hide under these covers a little longer today. Please let me stay numb and out of it. Please let me escape from it all."

So why did the rabbis in ancient times put the words *"Modeh ani"* into the early morning prayers? The phrase *"Modeh ani"* first appeared almost two thousand years ago in the beautiful morning prayer that says, *"Elohai neshamah shena-tata be, t'horah he,"* which in English is: "My God, the soul You placed within me is pure. You created it, You fashioned it, You breathed it into me, You safeguard it within me, and eventually You will take it from me and restore it in Time to Come. As long as the soul is within me, *Modeh ani,* I gratefully acknowledge You."

Then around 1600 a shortened twelve-word *"Modeh ani"* prayer began to appear in prayer books in Europe. The word *ani* means "I," but according to Reuven Hammer, author of *Entering Jewish Prayer,* there is no clear-cut way to translate *modeh* into English. The closest equivalent is "to gratefully acknowledge." Yet those words sound a bit awkward. Even in the "thank you for sharing" psychobabble of Southern California, where I've lived for the past twenty-three years since moving from the East Coast, we don't go around saying, "I gratefully acknowledge you."

If you look underneath the cumbersome English phrase "gratefully acknowledge" and just focus on the feeling of the Hebrew words *Modeh/Modah,* it's almost like the sensation of *kvelling,* a Yiddish word that means "to feel joy in your entire being." *Kvelling* expresses a sense of fullness or completeness because something wonderful is happening or because you feel loved and connected to a best friend, a beloved partner, or a child whose joyfulness makes you feel alive. My grandfather was troubled by stomach problems, hearing problems, and a pacemaker for his ailing heart—but when he would see my sister or me enter the room we could sense him *kvelling.* His eyes would light up, and his smile healed his aches and pains, at least for a moment.

The sense of fullness and excitement that makes a person feel like saying *"Modeh"* or *"Modah"* with grateful appreciation has a profound spiritual level as well. The words are saying to God or to the universe, "I feel alive and grateful," "I feel connected to a fullness that is beyond words." The same root word found in *Modeh* and *Modah* appears in several other important prayers in Judaism, such as the prayer of passionate thanks, *"Va'anakhnu kor-eem, oo-mish-takhavim oo-modim"*—"We bow the head and bend the knee in deep gratitude," which is stated during the Aleynu prayer near the end of the daily and Sabbath services.

The same hard-to-translate root word appears in the traditional prayer of thanks recited several times each weekday and on the Sabbath in the Amidah (standing up) prayer, which says, *"Modim anakh-nu lakh"*—"We gratefully thank You our God for all the blessings in our lives." The plural *modim,* the masculine singular *modeh,* and the feminine singular *modah* are more than just a polite "thank-you." They are the not-quite-adequate words we use for expressing our deep appreciation and joy for being alive.

Imagine yourself truly talking to God, to the creative force of the universe, or to the in-dwelling Presence of God referred to in Hebrew as Shekhinah (which according to Jewish mysticism connects your heart and soul to the hearts and souls of those around you). If you were connecting with Shekhinah or Divine Presence, what would it feel like to express what it means to you to have been given the gift of a pure soul that lives inside you? How would you convey your deep sense of gratefulness?

Outsmarting the Human Brain

At the point, first thing in the morning, when you and I are feeling groggy, with heavy eyelids, sour breath, and empty stomachs, Jewish spirituality offers us a chance to feel blessed that our souls have been restored and renewed for one more day. The exact instant you feel like insisting, "Let me go back to sleep," is when you're given an opportunity to talk directly with the loving Presence that connects all living things. What a radical idea!

As a psychologist I'd add that this early morning prayer is even more insightful because of a crucial discovery about how the human brain works. In 1927 at the University of Berlin, one of the first great female psychological researchers, Bluma Zeigarnik, was studying human perception in the hope of finding out how the brain decides what to focus on and what to ignore or overlook. She showed a large number of experimental volunteers a circle that was seven-eighths complete. Take a moment to look at the shape illustrated here and see what your eyes and your brain tend to focus on.

In a series of groundbreaking experiments Zeigarnik demonstrated that the human brain, which operates like a problem-solving machine, tends to focus more on the unfinished part of the circle. It's as though our brains are programmed to look at the problem, the interruption, or the deficiency and not at what's substantially correct or satisfying.

Later researchers called this the Zeigarnik effect, and it suggests that we human beings have a problem noticing what's going right in our lives. Our brains long to find something to criticize, something to worry about, something that's missing or interrupted. Is it any wonder your boss, your spouse, or even your own inner critic tends to dwell on what's not so good and seems to take for granted much of the time what's in good shape or what's already been achieved?

Having a problem-focused brain is both a blessing and a curse. It's a blessing to have a problem-solving machine that helps us look for unfinished tasks to be completed. But it's a curse in that our problem-focused brain won't let us feel satisfied, relaxed, or complete. Being human and possessing a problem-seeking brain means that at any given moment you're less likely to feel good about your life and more likely to feel, "No matter what I do it's never enough."

So the rabbis were trying to outsmart the human brain by asking us to begin each day with gratitude, wholeness, and connection to the miracle of being alive. The scholars and teachers who choreographed the morning prayers wanted us to enter the day by taking note of something important that our brains would normally ignore or take for granted. In essence, the "Modeh/Modah ani" prayer says, "Don't let your brain and your body keep you stuck in a life of problems, interruptions, and feelings of 'never enough.' For at least a moment each morning, send a surge of positive energy through your nerve passageways into your heart, stomach, hands, and legs. Give your weary body and soul the nourishment of noticing what a blessing it is to be renewed for another day. Especially if your life is hard, take a moment to experience the wonder of being a spiritual human being with a soul of purity and purpose that lives inside you."

Question 2
What Do You Believe It Means to Have a Soul?

If you want to pray with sincerity and say, *"Modeh or Modah ani"*—"Thank you for restoring and renewing my soul," you will also need to clarify what you mean by *soul*. When you say the word *soul*, what do you have in mind? Is it a physical entity that you can see with a microscope and that exists somewhere inside your brain? Is the soul an aura or a magnetic field that can't be seen with the untrained eye but can be picked up by certain parapsychological devices? Does it have a glow or an electrical frequency? Or is the word *soul* a metaphor that describes the nonphysical but spiritually real spark of divine energy contained within us? Are the souls of human beings somehow connected to a universal soul, a higher consciousness, or a divine mind, which we refer to as God? Or do you tend to believe there is no such thing as a soul—that we are nothing more than bodies with brains and that there is no spiritual reality beyond death?

In traditional Jewish belief, and especially in the mystical tradition of Judaism described in the writings of the Kabbalah (a series of "received wisdom" teachings that describe levels of reality beyond what the eyes can see), each of us has a multileveled, unified soul. One part is the *nefesh*—the breath or vital energy that animates our bodies at birth and pulses within us.

If you have ever seen a person during his or her final moments, you probably have a notion of what *nefesh* (breath/soul) means. At one moment a person is breathing in a labored fashion, and the soul or life force seems to be in the person's body. But then the breathing stops, and over a period of minutes you sense the soul has begun to depart from the physical body, which starts to resemble a shell that no longer contains the life force or soul.

I first witnessed this amazing phenomenon when I was twenty-three years old and watched a beloved relative die after a long illness. I recall the moment when the breathing stopped, the body began to cool, and the life force or *nefesh* seemed to be drifting out of the lifeless body.

In addition to the *nefesh*/life-force type of soul that you can almost perceive with your senses, there are at least two other levels of soul that are much harder to pinpoint. In Judaism, the *ruakh* is the intermediate level of soul. *Ruakh* describes the hidden force that raises the breath or spirit in our bodies by connecting us with the holy energies and wisdom of the *neshamah*, or higher levels of soul. The *neshamah* is an invisible but extremely powerful energy that links us with divine realms of higher consciousness, universal wisdom, and the unfolding of the cosmos.

If these words sound too strange for your rational mind, please be patient. Despite your healthy skepticism, you may have received glimpses of the *neshamah* soul. You might already have some clues for understanding what it means to have a higher self or a deep soul connection.

When Have You Experienced a Glimpse into Someone's Soul?

In the "Modeh/Modah ani" prayer, the level of soul we are thanking God for is the *neshamah*. I have found repeatedly that even the most skeptical and nonreligious individuals describe experiences that suggest a connection to this level of soul. For example, many people report an inner sense of "knowing" or seeing a person or event in their mind's eye a few minutes or days before that person or event showed up in their physical world. There are things we know in our souls that our brains can't seem to figure out.

When I was a student at Kenyon College in Ohio many years ago, I was close friends with a brilliant scientist, a strongly convinced atheist, who claimed there was no such thing as God or soul or universal mind. But one day this scientist woke up from a dream in which her mother was in a plane crash. The very next day her mother barely survived a plane disaster. My friend told me at the time, "I felt like I was connected somehow to a source of information that is beyond time and space, almost as if my soul was trying to tell me something that my rational mind cannot comprehend."

Some people feel a "soul connection" to a deceased loved one (a spouse, parent, grandparent, child, or friend whose presence is still felt at times). Or they feel a *bashert* (it was meant to be) "soul connection" with a certain person, a bond not just on the physical plane but on a spiritual level as well. Or we find truth in the statement "The eyes are the windows to the soul," because we have looked into someone's eyes and sensed that we can see his essence or spiritual purity.

If you've ever watched a baby being born or sat up with a sleeping child in the middle of the night, you probably have experienced moments of connecting with someone's soul or her pure essence. In your personal belief system, is it more than just an electromagnetic life force that animates this person? Is there also a connection to higher levels of consciousness, maybe even a spark of the Divine? Jewish tradition and the writings of the Kabbalah would say yes.

Looking for the Purpose of a Soul

If you close your eyes for a moment and say, *"Modeh/Modah ani*, I am so thankful my *neshamah*/soul is being renewed for another day," does it make you want to do something useful, positive, or purposeful with the day in front of you? Does thinking about your soul make you want to seek more meaning and connection in your daily life?

In the sixteenth century there was a great teacher named Rabbi Isaac Luria, whose talks about finding and fulfilling the purposes of your soul still inspire men and women. Luria, a master teacher of the Kabbalah, explained to his students that our task in life is to find and utilize the hidden holy sparks of light or divine energy that each of us carries in our soul. These sparks of holy wisdom and purpose come from the Creator, and our task is to find out what sparks or qualities of goodness we've been given. For example, you might be gifted with the ability to make people feel welcome or the ability to help someone who feels like an outsider. Or you might have the spark of being committed to justice and fairness, or the spark of being creative or innovative. By repairing ourselves and repairing the world, we bring these divine energies out from their coverings. By expressing and sharing our gifts, we raise up these energies to their Source.

For many Jews this is an inspiring vision of why we wake up in the morning and why our lives have purpose. Whether you accept Luria's vision as fact or as metaphor, it can give you a strong sense of purpose to see each day as a chance for *tikkun ha-nefesh* (repair of the soul) and *tikkun olam* (repair of the world). Many Jews from all branches of Judaism share a belief that an aspect of the Holy One lives within each human being and that we are God's "language" (that God speaks and acts in this world through human efforts of kindness, fairness, and purpose).

However, if you are skeptical about the existence of God or souls, this may be a difficult idea to embrace. If so, don't worry. You can still offer heartful thanks each morning that you are alive and renewed. You can honestly say, *"Modeh ani"* or *"Modah ani,"* to express your deep appreciation that your life force has been restored and renewed for another day. Being alive is remarkable in itself, regardless of what you believe is the source of that spark of vitality.

Using the Prayer to Be More Responsive to the Needs of Your Soul

One of the most profound benefits of saying the "Modeh/ Modah ani" prayer first thing in the morning is that it alerts your mind that throughout the day you will have one or more choice moments, when you can take advantage of opportunities to live with purpose or be oblivious to these opportunities. For instance, by expressing thanks first thing in the morning that you have a compassionate and purposeful soul, you are alerting your mind to be ready for any of the following actions that might be possible as the day unfolds:

> To express the creativity and generosity that you have been keeping inside but that your soul longs to express

> To give the kindness and warmth that you have been keeping inside but that your soul longs to give

> To fulfill the desire to be helpful, useful, and needed that you have been keeping inside but that your soul longs to fulfill

> To act on the curiosity and insightfulness that you have been keeping inside but that your soul longs to act on

In later chapters we will discuss in greater detail how to find and fulfill your purpose. For now let's just focus on the wake-up call that happens when you begin your day by alerting your mind to the importance of addressing the needs of your soul. As a psychologist I have seen repeatedly that when people start their day by saying, "Let me go back to sleep," "Let me stay numb or unconscious," or "Let me escape from the responsibilities in my life," it is far more likely that during the morning, afternoon, and evening they will feel tired, distracted, or unhappy. By contrast, when people start the day by calling upon their spiritual centers and saying, "Let me be aware of the needs of my soul today," they feel far more creativity, compassion, and inner strength through the rest of the day.

I can't force you to start using the "Modeh/Modah ani" prayer as a way to make each day more soul-satisfying. That's up to you. But if you have ever longed for a way to make your life a more meaningful expression of the longings of your soul, this prayer can help.

Question 3
When This Prayer Talks of God's Dependability, Does It Make You Wonder About Unanswered Prayers?

Now we come to the third and, for many people, the most confusing or difficult part of the "Modeh/Modah ani" prayer. The first part offers deep gratitude at waking up; the second part acknowledges that your soul is being renewed for another day with opportunities to have a purpose. The third and final section of the prayer says, *"Rabbah emunatekha,"* which usually is translated "You are dependable beyond measure." Some scholars translate it as "Great is Your faithfulness," because it comes from a verse in the Book of Lamentations (3:23) that says, "They are new each morning, great is Your faithfulness."

Let me ask you a controversial and personal question: Do you ever feel unsure of whether God is dependable and faithful? When you've been in a religious worship service, have you ever wondered about any of the prayers that say, "God is dependable, God is faithful, God provides for your every need, and God rewards those who follow God's ways"? When you've gone through an intense situation, do you wonder if God is really listening or if God truly intervenes on your behalf?

In order to pray with sincerity, *"Modeh/Modah ani . . . rabbah emunatekha,* You are dependable beyond measure," you first need to examine what is meant by a "reliable Presence" in your daily life. Otherwise your prayers will feel empty or you'll be holding a concern that maybe God isn't as faithful or dependable as the prayer says.

I've found in my counseling sessions with even the most devout individuals, including some rabbis and their spouses who discussed their inner life with me, that many of them have moments of doubt or uncertainty about whether or not they can depend on God. Even the most observant Jews sometimes find themselves asking, "Where was God's faithfulness during the Holocaust? Where was God's dependability when my loved one was ill or when my infant died? How can we say God provides for our every need when there is so much hunger and cruelty still in the world?"

So if you have ever asked these difficult questions, please don't feel like you're alone or you're doing something forbidden. I urge you to take note of the fact that in Judaism it's permissible to argue with God, to ask tough questions, and to be honest about your internal struggles. The literal meaning of the word Israelite is "the one who wrestles and strives with God." If you were raised in a family or religious school that forbade you to express your concerns about complex questions such as "Is God dependable?" please know that some of the most respected Jewish teachers, scholars, and leaders in history had moments of doubt and uncertainty.

Choosing Between Two Notions of "Dependable"

There are at least two belief systems within Judaism about why God acts in mysterious ways and often seems not to intervene in particular situations. You might agree or disagree with one or both of these views. But in considering these positions, you will be engaging in the most basic activity of Jewish spirituality and prayer—you will be wrestling with God.

One viewpoint, often called process theology and discussed in detail in Rabbi Harold Kushner's book *When Bad Things Happen to Good People,* suggests that God's love and concern are dependable but God's influence is at times limited. According to this view, God is a loving Presence or Source of holiness that we can connect with at any time but that cannot override human free will or natural forces that the Creator set in motion long ago. In other words, God can't stop a hurricane, an earthquake, or an illness because these natural forces have both physical properties and a degree of randomness that are part of the Creator's design for them. In the process theology view, God cares deeply and inspires people to develop cures, to act with generosity, or to respond with kindness to the tragedies and vulnerabilities that are a part of life.

In addition, the process theology view says that God can't stop human beings from mistreating one another. Nor can God prevent a Holocaust, a genocide, or an "ethnic cleansing," except by inspiring people to take action to stop such human cruelty. Part of God's creation is that human beings have free will, including the freedom to do evil. God can only teach, inspire, and attempt to awaken our divine sparks so that we will fight against injustice and treat with compassion those who have been victimized. God depends on human beings to finish the job of creation and to repair the problems that human free will and powerful natural forces sometimes inflict on this world. If you look at God as a source of healing but not as the cause of our suffering, you are agreeing with the process theology viewpoint.

The second belief system held by many Jews about God's dependability is that God is *not* limited but is all-powerful. If God chooses not to intervene in a situation, or if God does intervene and that intervention causes suffering on one level of reality, it is because of unknown factors and unseen levels of reality we human beings cannot fully understand. This more traditional view of God as an omnipotent source of guidance and justice also sees God as a loving Presence, even if at times God's love appears to be stern or mysterious. For example, according to some Kabbalistic teachings, if an innocent child dies at a young age, it might be because an all-powerful God has sent this child's pure soul into the world for a short time (possibly to open certain people's hearts and minds or to inspire certain people to come up with a cure or proper funding for dealing with a terrible ailment).

We human beings can't know the mind of God or the realities of the divine realms that are working out scenarios for us on Earth. Our task is not to close our hearts when we are troubled by what God has given us but rather to find ways to heal our own brokenness and to bring about repair and healing in the world around us.

If you have ever prayed by asking God to intervene in the illness of someone you cared about, or to help you solve a problem in your life, you may have been connecting with a sense of God as an all-powerful, ever-present force that actively guides the world. If your prayer seemed to be unanswered, your response might have been, "I don't know the ways of God but yet I trust that God has a reason."

Working Through the Anger

Whether you think of God as limited or all-powerful, you probably have experienced moments where you felt that God didn't seem to respond to your prayers for help. At those moments you may have felt upset or distant from God. For many Jews this feeling of estrangement from God has been most troublesome as a result of the murder of more than six million Jews (as well as many other innocent souls) during the Nazi onslaught sixty years ago. How does a survivor of the Holocaust (or, in my own case, a second-generation child of a Holocaust survivor who lost many of his relatives) offer prayers of *"Modeh ani"* to a God who is *"rabbah emunatekha"*—dependable and faithful?

Many theories have been proposed about what a loving and caring God might have been doing while so many innocent adults and children were being rounded up, shot, gassed, and tortured during World War II. There are no easy answers. One Holocaust survivor, the award-winning author and activist Elie Wiesel, has suggested that it is normal to feel angry with God about the Holocaust and at the same time to love God and grieve with God over the deaths of so many beloved people. Wiesel recently wrote a Yom Kippur statement regarding some of his feelings about God. This statement can provide some profound insights.

Wiesel writes, "Master of the Universe, let us make up. It is time. How long can we go on being angry? After all, Auschwitz was not something that came down ready-made from heaven. It was conceived by men, implemented by men, staffed by men. And their sin was not only to destroy us but You as well." He continues, "Ought we not to think of your pain, too? Watching your children suffer at the hands of your other children, haven't you also suffered? Let us make up, Master of the Universe, in spite of everything that happened. It is unbearable to be divorced from you so long."

If you or someone in your life has felt betrayed or ignored by God, it may take a long time for that broken trust to heal. My hope is that you or this person will consider taking steps toward healing the rift with the mysterious Source of all that is. Like Elie Wiesel, many individuals have been upset with God or life yet have decided that "in spite of everything that happened it is unbearable to be divorced from you so long."

Opening up again spiritually may require a rethinking of what you believe about God. Maybe God's dependability and faithfulness are not about God rushing in and taking over 100 percent to reverse humanity's actions. Possibly God's being "*rabbah emunatekha*"—dependable beyond measure—has to do with other ways in which the Divine Presence is there for us and assists us in living our lives.

What Can You Depend On?

A few years ago I conducted a workshop on spirituality and psychology with a group of men and women from a diversity of professions and varying degrees of religious or spiritual identification. In one of the exercises I asked the participants to explore what types of faithfulness and reliability they experience from God or the universe on a daily basis. Here are a few of the responses. See which ring true for you or stir up ideas about what you can depend on each day:

"I can depend on the most beautiful sunrises and sunsets that happen daily even if I forget to go look at them."

"I can depend on my lungs and heart keeping my breath going and my internal organs functioning within my body even if I'm not paying attention to it. Something created that in a miraculous fashion."

"I can depend on the ocean waves coming in and going out no matter how good or frustrating a day I've had."

"Since I'm a creative person, I depend on God for frequent inspiration and ideas that come from a deeper place than my rational mind."

"As a holistic healer, I depend on God for thousands of amazing herbs, plants, and natural elements that were put on Earth by a Creative Force that wanted us to unlock the secrets of nature."

"I can depend on God inspiring me as a parent to be loving to my kids, even when they are difficult."

"Sometimes when I'm driving in traffic and I'm lost in my thoughts, I depend on God or some loving force to give me a quick jolt of awareness that saves me from crashing into another car who suddenly put his brakes on."

"Every time I look into the eyes of someone I love, I feel connected to God's generosity and faithfulness."

"I occasionally depend on God to give me guidance or strength for dealing with the most difficult moments of my life."

"I depend on God as the reference point for helping me remember to do the right thing in situations where I'm tempted to mess up . . . and this solid reference point can't be seduced, conned, or deceived."

"I depend on God to be a silent partner I will never fully understand, but that I believe is a force in my life and my interactions each day."

"Sometimes when I'm having a hard day, some person (often a stranger) does something kind or considerate and it begins to turn my day around. These are the moments when I feel God's Presence working through the heartfelt actions of human beings."

"I depend on God to be mysterious at times, seemingly unavailable at times, but always there in my heart when I take a few moments to slow down and ask for strength."

If any of these statements are sometimes true in your life, can you thank God each morning for being "dependable beyond measure"? Can you work through the hidden distrust or resentment that has kept you separate from God's Presence in your life? This is the challenge each of us faces in this post-Holocaust era—to notice God's generous contributions to our everyday lives. If each morning while saying the "Modeh/ Modah ani" prayer you remember at least one thing for which you are grateful, it will help you feel more connected to the spiritual gifts you carry in your soul—the gifts that God or life has given you to share with others.

Saying the Prayer with Deeper Intention

Now that we've explored some of the intricacies and deeper levels of meaning of the "Modeh/Modah ani" prayer, let's look again at the words. Here is the Hebrew version and the English translation that you can say first thing in the morning to reenergize your soul and connect with your higher purpose:

Men:	Modeh ani l'fanekha	
Women:	Modah ani l'fanekha	I am so thankful in front of You,
Both men and women:	melekh* khai v'kayam	Ruling Force of life and existence,
	sheh-hekheh-zarta be nishmatee b'khemla	Who restores and renews my soul with compassion.
	rabbah emunatekha.	You are dependable beyond measure.

*Some prayer books translate *melekh* as "king," while others avoid the male anthropomorphic imagery by translating *melekh* as "sovereign," "ruling force," or "preeminent One."

If you have trouble remembering all the words at first, you can start out by simply saying, *"Modeh* (or) *Modah ani"* in Hebrew and then say in English, "I am so thankful in front of You, Ruling Force of life, for restoring and renewing my soul with such dependability." What's important is the *kavannah,* or intention, that you carry in your heart. Are you willing to be grateful for having a remarkable soul? Do you want to address the needs of your soul today? Do you long for a connection to the Source Who breathed this soul into you and sustains it each day and night?

In Your Own Words

What else do you want to say first thing in the morning to renew your best self and reenergize your sense of higher purpose? What words or feelings would you like to consider for a moment before opening your eyes and getting busy with the day ahead of you?

At the end of each chapter in this book, I will explore in a brief section how to develop your own prayers and wordings for the things you want to communicate with God or the things you want to say to the part of yourself that needs to be awakened. Almost two thousand years ago, as far back as the Jerusalem Talmud (a collection of insights and commentaries on Jewish law and teachings), Rabbi Yose advised, "Let there be a novelty in your prayer every day." Otherwise, you fall into empty habits and meaningless repetitions.

According to the well-known Orthodox rabbi, physicist and scholar Aryeh Kaplan, author of the fascinating book *Jewish Meditation: A Practical Guide,* "There seems to be a feeling that Jewish prayer must be in Hebrew, in a prescribed manner, with a predetermined wording. Many Jews are surprised to learn that there is an unbroken tradition of spontaneous prayer in the Jewish religion. Although many sources discuss spontaneous prayer, one Jewish leader gave it a central role in his teachings: Rabbi Nachman of Bratslav." Kaplan continues, "Rabbi Nachman was a great-grandson of the Baal Shem Tov (the Master of the Good Name who founded the Hasidic movement in Poland in the eighteenth century). The Baal Shem taught that every individual could attain a strong personal relationship with God. Rabbi Nachman expanded this concept, teaching that the most powerful method to attain such a relationship with God is personal prayer in one's own native language."

So what do *you* want to say to the mysterious Source within you and above you first thing in the morning: Your hopes for the day? Your gratitude for the people and blessings that are part of your life right now? Your frustrations and your need for help and support? Your desire to have a good day and not be swept up by distractions or bad habits that will leave you feeling empty? Your longing to be of service to God and to do something to heal yourself or the world around you?

It's up to you. I can't tell you what to say, I can only recommend that talking with God first thing in the morning—silently or out loud—can make a huge difference in how you will respond to what life presents you that day. Here's one example of how someone began to develop her own words for awakening her spiritual side each morning.

Sheri is a highly educated divorced woman in her thirties who grew up in a secular Jewish home, where prayer was considered "old-fashioned" and "irrelevant." According to Sheri, "Like many other parents, my folks let me know that they'd be furious if I married a non-Jew, but they also never talked to me about God or encouraged me on how to be a spiritual person."

When Sheri came in for counseling after the breakup of a six-month relationship, she admitted, "I've been successful in my work life, but there's this longing in my soul for a deeper sense of connection to something beyond work. Maybe it's a relationship I'm looking for. Or maybe it's something in addition to a partner and a family. I feel like I want to explore who I am on a deeper level and to find out what my true purposes in life might be."

Over the next several months Sheri worked hard on her relationship issues and how to find and sustain a quality partnership. In addition, she began to explore how to make each day more spiritual and more meaningful. She experimented with different prayers and morning rituals. Gradually she came to realize that "the Modah ani prayer tends to center me and strengthen me each day when I remember to say it."

She admits, "I haven't told my parents yet that I'm doing this because they'd think I was losing my mind. My father especially would say something like, 'What are you, some kind of Holy Roller all of a sudden? That stuff is all nonsense.'"

Nevertheless, Sheri continued to use prayers as a way of starting her day in a more soulful manner. She comments, "I still have moments of doubt and uncertainty, but in the morning I imagine myself talking directly with the Shekhinah, the silent and loving Presence of God that I vaguely sense deep inside me. It's hard to describe, but I feel like I'm connecting into my true essence when I start the day in a spiritual and purposeful frame of mind."

After saying the "Modah ani" prayer in Hebrew and in English, Sheri usually offers a spontaneous short prayer. Each day the words are slightly different, but they are always sincere and genuine. Here is one of Sheri's prayers:

Dear God,

I want to feel connected to You today.

I want to be open to Your support and Your guidance.

There's something else I need, and it's hard for me to ask this.

I need You to help me open up this heart of mine that has been closed for far too long.

Show me how to be a loving person today and how to let in warmth from others.

Please don't let me be too busy to let some love in today.

Amen.

A few months after Sheri began saying these prayers each morning, she met someone who turned out to be her *bashert,* her soul mate. I've seen the two of them on several occasions, and I think they have a good chance of being together for a lifetime. As Sheri told me recently, "I prayed numerous times for assistance to help me open up and receive love and warmth. It looks like my prayers have come true."

Once again, I cannot promise that saying "Modeh ani" or "Modah ani," along with a spontaneous heartful prayer each morning, will result in a particular outcome. This is not about guarantees. But if you want to open up your consciousness to what your soul longs for, this prayer can be extremely helpful. I believe adding this ritual to your wake-up routine can affect your life in positive ways—some changes you might be able to see and some changes that are beyond understanding.

CHAPTER TWO

A Prayer to Help You Refocus When You're Feeling Stressed or Distracted

Barookh Atah Adonai	Blessed are You, Eternal One,
Eloheinu melekh ha-olam	Pulsing Source of all that exists in the world,
asheyr kid'shanu b'mitz-votav	Who guides us on ways to become holy,
vitzi-vanu al netilat yadayim.	And Who inspires us to lift our hands (to raise up our actions and be of service).

Have there been moments when you realized time is slipping by and something of importance keeps getting pushed aside? It's remarkable how we human beings come up with so many wonderful goals, dreams, and good intentions. Yet at the end of the day, do you sometimes look back and ask, "What happened? Why didn't I get to what I'd hoped to do today? I let the time pass without focusing on the very thing I care about most."

This chapter offers a practical method to get back on track, to make sure you don't let too much time slip by. It's about living your life with a stronger commitment to following through on what you cherish most and sticking with what you know in your heart is your higher purpose.

What Distracts You?

In order to improve your daily effectiveness, it's important to examine what happens each day that diverts you from your good intentions. For instance, have you ever gotten up in the morning with good ideas for making the day productive and meaningful, but within minutes your energy shifted? Perhaps your mind couldn't focus because there were too many things on your schedule. Or by the time you attended to all the mundane chores of your morning routine you lost your connection to what you really ought to be doing. Or you'd gotten interrupted repeatedly, either by your own thoughts or by demands and distractions from other people. From listening to numerous patients and friends over the years, I've noticed that following through on your most heartfelt priorities each day is one of the toughest challenges we face. There are so many daily stresses and distractions—it's hard to stay focused on what matters most.

For example, a creative graphics designer and visual artist named Daniel came to me for counseling because for years he had found himself unable to bring to completion many of his best creative ideas. As he told me with ironic humor during his initial session: "I know how to make an exquisite to do list each day. But my problem is focusing and following through. Nearly every day, after a quick burst of focused energy, I find myself getting distracted and slipping into a funk. It's extremely frustrating because I've got a lot of good ideas I want to bring to fruition, but I somehow get off track each day, and then it's hard to start the creative juices flowing again."

Since Daniel had for many years been interested in spiritual books and topics, he sometimes described his productivity dilemma in almost mystical terms. He commented, "Every so often when I take a look at my life, I sense that I'm not fully using the gifts and opportunities I've been given by God or whatever makes us the way we are. I feel there must be a reason why I've been given this much passion for visual design. Yet for the most part I'm not following through on that passion."

Because Daniel seemed open to a spiritual perspective, I asked him if he would be willing to try out a spiritually based method for dealing with his daily distractibility and lack of follow-through. He replied, "If it works, I'll try anything."

The following is what I recommended to Daniel because it has worked successfully for many men and women I've counseled who have great ideas but insufficient follow-through. You will need to test it out for yourself to see if it helps you move closer to your full potential as a caring and creative human being.

A Cleansing Prayer

In Jewish spiritual practice there's a prayer that you can use whenever your mind gets fragmented or distracted. It's called "Netilat yadayim," which literally means "to raise or lift up your hands." On my own and with some of my counseling clients, I've experimented for several years with this easy-to-use but profound prayer as a creative way to get back on track midmorning or midafternoon with what really matters most in life. Here are the steps you can take when you are starting to lose your focus.

1. If you notice your mind is cloudy or your plans for the day have gotten pushed aside, take a moment to go to a nearby washroom, kitchen sink, or other place where you've set aside a pitcher of water.

2. Stop for a few seconds so you can set your intention on restarting the day and reconnecting with your deeper spiritual self. Then take a deep breath in and out as you say the traditional words of transformation in the "Netilat yadayim" prayer. Here are the original Hebrew words along with a modern translation.

Barookh Atah	Blessed are You,
Adonai Eloheinu	Eternal One,
melekh ha-olam	Pulsing Source of all that exists in the world,
asheyr kid'shanu b'mitz-votav	Who guides us on ways to become holy,
vitzi-vanu al netilat yadayim.	And Who inspires us to lift our hands (to raise up our actions and be of service).

(You may need to read it from a piece of paper until you begin to know it by heart.)

3. After you say the prayer you can either pour cool water three times over each hand with a ladle or small container or soak your hands under cool or slightly warm tap water. Be sure to consider that the water is cleansing you not only physically but spiritually.

4. As the water runs over your hands, raise them gently in a receptive posture, with palms up and your small fingers touching. Take another deep breath in and out as you complete the ritual.

What the Words Mean on a Deeper Level

If you look deeper into the Hebrew words and mystical teachings about this unusual prayer, you will discover the hidden power of this ritual for transforming your blocked energy. You will begin to understand why many scholars and rabbis over the centuries have stated repeatedly that this prayer is *not* about washing physical germs off your hands—rather it's about aligning yourself with your true purpose for being of service that day in your own unique manner. As far back as the thirteenth century, a scholar named Rabbi Samson ben Zadok listed twelve times of day when you might use this prayer to raise your energy. First let's look at each of the words of the prayer to see how they relate to you personally.

The opening phrase, *"Barookh Atah Adonai Eloheinu, melekh ha-olam, asheyr kid'shanu b'mitz-votav,"* is one you might recognize. It's used in many important prayers, including the Friday night candle lighting, the Chanukah menorah lighting, and numerous other occasions when we bless and celebrate holy moments. There are many ways of translating these words. Specifically, the first four words, *"Barookh Atah Adonai Eloheinu,"* usually get translated, "Praised art Thou, Lord our God," which for many people is the most familiar and respectful way of starting a conversation with the Infinite One. In other prayer books you will see, "Blessed is the Lord thy God."

Yet some people don't feel comfortable with a word like "Lord" when talking to the loving Presence, the Shekhinah, which many experience as a "still small voice within." For many men and women today, "Praised art Thou, Lord our God" and "Blessed is the Lord thy God" sound distant and stiff, as though addressing a white-bearded, anthropomorphic father figure. That's why I offer a more personal and still respectful translation, "Blessed are You, Eternal One," recognizing that this, too, cannot adequately put in words the mysterious essence of the One with whom we long to connect. Please use whichever translation you feel is closest to the way you would like to speak to the infinite creative force we refer to as God.

The second phrase, *"melekh ha-olam,"* usually gets translated "King of the universe," a bold and courageous metaphor in ancient and medieval times, when most human beings were required to worship mortal kings while instead Jewish men and women worshiped only the immortal "King of the universe." But since most of us no longer are commanded to bow down to royalty, the term "King of the universe" might not draw you in. So *melekh ha-olam* can also be translated accurately as "Sovereign," "Protector," "Ruling Force," "Pulsing Universe," or "Source of all that is." You'll need to decide what metaphor feels most inspiring for how you want to relate to a higher power who cares about your well-being. I offer the words "Pulsing Source of all that exists in the world" because they suggest God as a source of wisdom, compassion, and strength you seek to connect with in a prayer.

The third phrase, *"asheyr kid'shanu b'mitz-votav,"* is often translated "Who sanctifies us with Your commandments." But the word *mitz-votav* can also mean "ways of being holy," "ways of connecting with God," or "ways of bringing goodness into the world."

Look into your own heart to find the English phrases that will bring you closest to a connection with the mysterious Being that dwells on high and lives deep within us. If the traditional phrasings speak to your soul, please use them. If the modern interpretations bring you closer to your spiritual connection, know that many rabbis and scholars support these translations.

If you are uncertain about which English words feel "right," you can consult your own most trusted teachers, rabbis, and written sources to find the prayer language that works for your spiritual path. What's most important is not to give up or shut down because a particular translation offends you or leaves you cold. To be an Israelite, to "wrestle and strive with God," means to keep questioning the words and rituals until you find what opens up your heart and allows you to feel a connection to your spirituality.

Exploring the Profound Usefulness of This Prayer

Finally, we get to *"vitzi-vanu al netilat yadayim,"* which is often mistranslated "Who commands us to wash our hands." Clearly, *yadayim* is the plural form of *yad,* which means "hand." But according to most Hebrew scholars, the word *netilat* comes from Aramaic, the language spoken in ancient Palestine, and literally means "to lift, to raise, to bear or hold." That's why a more accurate translation of *vitzi-vanu al netilat yadayim* is "Who inspires us to lift our hands."

To understand what "lift your hands" means from a spiritual perspective, let's consider an important clue found in the classic text *Kitzur Shulchan Aruch* (Abridged Code of Jewish Ritual Observance), written in 1870 by Rabbi Solomon Ganzfried. Notice that the Hebrew root word *avodah* (which means "to be of service") appears several times as the key reason for the hands being raised and cleansed.

Rabbi Ganzfried wrote, "To serve *(la-avodat)* the Creator, Blessed be the Name, therefore a person must be sanctified and wash his [or her] hands from a vessel, just as a *Kohein* [Jewish priest] washed his hands each day from the special basin located in the Temple prior to his service *(avodato).* This washing is indicated in the Scripture (Psalm 26, lines 6 and 7), as it is said, 'I will wash my hands in purity and I will encircle Your altar to proclaim a sound of thanks.'"

Take a moment to look at the three types of "giving service" Ganzfried says this prayer will allow you to do:

1. To set your intention that you want to *be of service* to the Creator

2. To imagine yourself like a high priest at the Temple preparing for *a service*

3. To move and speak in a way that *serves up an offering* to the One who gave you your gifts

Rabbi Ganzfried and most scholars say the "Netilat Yadayim" prayer can help you raise up your reason for living each day. Instead of just "getting by" in life, you have the chance to take action for a higher purpose, to experience *avodah* (being of service).

Avodah is one of those fascinating Hebrew words that can mean several things at once. Just as *shalom* means "hello," "good-bye," "peace," "wholeness," and "completeness" all at the same time, *avodah* possesses several simultaneous meanings that fit together in a profound way.

On the one hand, *avodah* means "to work" or "to take action." But it also means "to pray, to worship, to make an offering of thanks." In addition it can mean "to serve" or "be of service." If you put these various definitions together, you suddenly have the awareness that the purpose of daily work is not drudgery or cash flow but rather offering up your services and your talents for a higher purpose. You also are reminded that prayer and worship are not escapes from reality but rather are connected strongly to taking action in the world and bringing about the best in yourself and others.

How Would You Like to Be of Service?

Each of us defines what we mean by *avodah* in a slightly different manner. What kind of service comes to mind when you think of lifting up your actions for a higher purpose? What kind of offering to the Creator or to your corner of the universe would feel meaningful and worthwhile to you? If the "Netilat Yadayim" prayer were to help you personally overcome procrastination and assist you in getting back on track each day, with what type of "service" would you like it to help you follow through? Here are some possibilities to consider.

1. Would you like this prayer to help you be more focused and creative on a particular project on which you've been stalling for too long?

2. Would you like this hand-washing ritual to help you remember to be of service to someone who needs your strength and compassion? For example, a child with special needs, an aging family member or neighbor, a spouse who's been feeling neglected, an employee, co-worker, or customer who needs to receive the best you have to offer?

3. Would you like this prayer to remind you to be more generous or involved with a specific nonprofit activity, or an effort to eliminate a painful injustice or type of mistreatment that you've wanted to do something about?

4. Would you like this ritual to help you become more open
   and responsive each day when strangers, friends, or family
   ask you for assistance or caring?

5. Would you like this prayer to help you deepen your connection to God and to your partnership in helping to repair
   some aspect of God's creation?

On both a physical and an emotional level, there is something profound and beautiful about saying "Netilat Yadayim"
while letting the water run over your hands and contemp-
lating how to be of service. If you remember each day when
you are feeling stuck or distracted that this type of spiritual
reawakening is possible, then you will have a chance to dramatically improve your follow-through on things that truly
matter.

"I Began to See My Daily
Activities in a Whole New Light"

Daniel used the "Netilat Yadayim" prayer for a while before
he noticed much change in his outlook or energy. He says,
"The first time I said the prayer and washed my hands it felt
uncomfortable and unfamiliar. The way I spoke the words at
first seemed stiff and awkward. I became self-conscious that
I, a somewhat skeptical Jew who had studied Buddhism and
other Eastern religions when I couldn't find my spiritual
connection to Judaism, was all of a sudden performing a very
ancient Jewish ritual." But after a few days Daniel found (as
did many of my counseling clients) that the prayer began to

shift his energy from distractibility and made it easier for him to focus.

He explains, "I can't say whether it's the physical act of putting my hands in soothing water that gets my brain out of distractibility and into a more creative and productive frame of mind. Or it might be the words I was taking to heart—I really started to think about what it means to be preparing myself for being of service and following through for a higher purpose. I took a few moments to consider exactly what might be my particular way of offering up my talents for a positive result. I realized that when I help people improve their graphics, their promotion materials, or their web sites, I'm hopefully contributing to good not only for my customers but also for the thousands of men, women, and children who are going to be impacted by what my clients do for them."

Daniel continues, "Sometimes I'm alone for hours with my computer, and I don't get to see whether I'm being of service to any actual human beings. But occasionally I get a clear sense that I *am* using my gifts in a way that makes a difference to someone. Last week one of my customers wrote me an e-mail and said she appreciated what I did for them not only because it made her company look good in the marketplace but, more importantly, because of the way I treated her and her co-workers."

The e-mail said, "Every other computer graphics person we've dealt with talked down to us because we don't know computers as well as they do. But you spoke to us like we were human beings worthy of respect. That inspired us to develop some of the most creative and dynamic design elements we've ever come up with on a project. For that we thank you."

Daniel smiled as he told me about the e-mail and explained, "Things that used to seem like opposites—work versus spirituality, making a living versus doing good and treating people respectfully—these don't seem so far apart any longer. For some reason, when I take a moment once or twice a day to rinse my hands and offer up a prayer about being of service, it centers me and allows me to be more productive and caring than I've been in the past."

He admits, "I still have a slight tendency to get lost in my thoughts. But when I started to connect each work assignment to how I want to be of service, I began to see my daily activities in a whole new light. And using this ancient prayer ritual once or twice a day has made me at least 60 percent better at staying focused and getting back on track when I do get distracted. That's a big improvement over how I was before I started using this prayer."

How Do You Feel About Lifting Up Your Hands?

Even though I've seen repeatedly that the "Netilat Yadayim" prayer is highly effective for helping people focus and follow through on what matters most to them, I've also found many men and women are reluctant to try it out. Approximately one-third of the people with whom I discussed this prayer told me that they felt hesitant or uncomfortable with the idea of "raising up" their hands.

For example, Joyce is an extremely intelligent retired social worker who grew up in a nonreligious home with two parents who were left-wing intellectuals. She says, "I've always felt somewhat Jewish. Both of my parents were raised in Orthodox homes, and my social work career was influenced by the Jewish values I heard each year at my friends' Passover seders about reaching out and caring for the immigrant and the stranger in need. But prayer and belief in God were not a part of my upbringing. Nor was religion very important in my adult life, since I was married to a Unitarian and we made an agreement to raise our kids to be thoughtful and kind but not to be any particular faith."

She continues, "So even though I definitely agree with you that I need a technique for overcoming procrastination and getting myself to focus better on some of the projects I want to do now that I'm retired, I'm not sure if I'm comfortable raising up my hands to an invisible God."

Joyce also confided that she was a little nervous about admitting her religious skepticism to me. She explained, "My only other therapist was thirty years ago, and he was an egotistical male who interpreted any disagreement by his patients as 'stubborn resistance.' Plus I've always been concerned that when you admit to someone of faith that you're a skeptic, they tend to start arguing with you. Or they shun you and treat you like you're some kind of pathetic half-human, which I don't believe I am."

I was glad Joyce felt comfortable enough to be this honest. As I explained to her, when someone is genuine and admits how they struggle with doubt or hesitation regarding therapy techniques or spiritual questions, I welcome their comments. In fact, there is something very Jewish and psychologically healthy about having the freedom to discuss and wrestle with your inner doubts and frustrations. I asked her, though, "On a scale of zero to 100, what percentage of you is sure there's no such thing as a loving Presence? And what percentage of you has some curiosity or even a small sense of belief in a mysterious source of wisdom and compassion, maybe even in a God that you argue with or get disappointed with from time to time?"

Joyce smiled and commented, "Are you asking if I ever get mad at God? Of course, I get mad at God every time I see injustice in the world. But if you want to know whether I think there's a God Who will help me if I'm in trouble? I don't know. I'd say I'm at least 80 percent skeptical."

I thanked Joyce again for her honesty, and I told her about one of my favorite teachers, Rabbi Zalman Schachter-Shalomi of Boulder, Colorado, who has an interesting way of looking at doubt and disbelief. Reb Zalman suggests that if you find an aspect of God or religion that you don't believe in, it's not necessary to say, "I don't believe in the whole thing." Rather, it's more accurate to say, "There's a part of me—maybe 80 percent of my brain—that doesn't believe in that aspect. But there's another part of me—maybe 20 percent of my brain— that is curious and wonders if possibly some of that stuff about an infinite source of wisdom and compassion might be true."

Rather than calling yourself a believer or a nonbeliever, Reb Zalman recommends giving yourself permission to be in an ongoing process of exploring your spiritual curiosity and connection. At one moment you might be feeling 10 percent connected to your faith and 90 percent skeptical. A good option at that moment is to say a prayer, perform a ritual, or engage in an act of kindness to open your heart to maybe a 30 percent connection to your spiritual side. Or if there are moments when you're feeling 80 percent connected to your spiritual self, then your next challenge might be to find out what it feels like to be 90 percent connected to a holy way of being.

With regard to lifting up your hands, Reb Zalman and many other teachers would say to give yourself permission to be honest about exactly where you are in the process. If it makes you feel 60 percent self-conscious or skeptical to raise your hands in prayer, so be it. That doesn't make you a bad person or destroy your relationship with God. But then take a deep breath and try again, to see if you can become maybe 51 percent aligned with the Divine Presence and only 49 percent skeptical as you raise your hands a few inches higher to offer your services to the One who needs your partnership in repairing the world.

Even if you experience an incredible moment when you feel 100 percent in alignment with God, you might be right back to 60 percent skeptical the next moment. Don't despair— this drawing closer, then losing touch, and finally drawing closer again is what it means to be a human being on a spiritual path. It's not an all-or-nothing activity but rather a daily process of seeking a way back to your highest and most productive spiritual self.

When I looked at Joyce in the middle of our conversation about degrees of skepticism, tears were welling up in her eyes. I asked her what she was feeling. She explained: "This is the first time in my life I've ever felt permission to be exactly where I am in relationship to this whole God question. I always felt like I was going to be criticized for doing it wrong. There's so much judgmentalness when it comes to talking about faith and religion. I've often been a little bit curious about all this. But I've never felt safe talking about it because of how rigid and opinionated everyone gets. Not just the people who are dogmatic believers but also the men and women, my parents included, who are just as dogmatic in their disbelief."

After that conversation Joyce decided to experiment using the "Netilat Yadayim" prayer during the times midmorning and midafternoon when she was losing focus or slipping into distractibility or procrastination. As she later reported: "The first few times I tried it, I felt foolish because I was so self-conscious raising my hands a few inches into the air and hoping to connect with a guiding force I'd never really trusted very much. But then there was a morning last week when I definitely needed this prayer to work. I had wanted to put out a huge mailing to organize a volunteer network of retired social workers who could help get services for low-income single moms who were falling through the cracks of the system.

"I'd been procrastinating on this mailing for almost a month. Then last week I was so frustrated when I realized I'd wasted another two hours that morning getting interrupted by all sorts of lesser projects and I wasn't focusing on the mailing. So I picked myself up from my desk, went to the rest room, and said the prayer with the water running over my fingers. Then I raised my hands at least six inches and said silently, 'Please God, help me to focus. You've given me all this fire and commitment for doing good in the world. Now help me to follow through and make it happen.'"

Joyce told me this was the first time she'd ever felt a prayer deeply in her heart. She commented, "I had always thought prayer was nothing more than people who don't want to take responsibility for their lives asking some deity to do it for them. Now for the first time I realized that prayer is not a cop-out. Admitting to God exactly what's going on is a way of taking responsibility for what you really care about in life while asking for strength and guidance so you can follow through and do the right thing."

Joyce concluded, "It felt strange and rather liberating to be asking a loving Presence for support after all these years. With renewed energy, I marched out of the rest room feeling extremely motivated, sat down at my desk, and put in almost two hours of uninterrupted work getting out that mailing. I felt so alive, and I've used the prayer several times since to get that passionate flow happening again."

In Your Own Words

Picture yourself midmorning or midafternoon feeling distracted or unproductive, even though there are important things you know you need to accomplish. This would be an ideal moment to see if the "Netilat Yadayim" prayer helps you lift up your energy and your ability to follow through. Now ask yourself, What words do you want to say to God or to the universe, or to the soul within you? What words do you think will raise your vitality and your creativity at this crucial moment?

Over the years I've heard many personalized versions of this prayer from friends, counseling clients, teachers, and rabbis. Here is one of my favorites, which I hope will inspire you or someone you care about to talk honestly about what's blocking the creative flow and what might open it up again.

This version was given to me by Jennifer, a highly sensitive and intense fifteen-year-old who showed up reluctantly for counseling because her mother threatened to "ground her for life" if she didn't. At her initial session Jennifer made it clear she wasn't a great fan of psychotherapy: she called her mother a "manipulative witch," she referred to her father as a "complete dork," she asked me if I minded being bald, and she nervously twirled her reddish brown hair with its purple, orange, and green streaks.

Jennifer also admitted she had trouble concentrating in school and had fallen into the habit of saving her homework assignments to the last minute and putting things off beyond the deadlines set by her teachers, whom she referred to as "sadistic control freaks." When I asked her if there was anyone or anything she did feel she could respect or admire, she looked up and said, "God."

She seemed surprised when I took her seriously and asked, "So tell me what it's like trying to connect with God." Like many teenagers and young adults who appear to be rebellious and cynical, Jennifer slowly revealed that she possessed a rich inner life. Over the next few weeks she told me some of the things she wrote about each night in her private journal. She admitted she held a secret wish of becoming an environmental lawyer and preventing companies from poisoning the air and water. She also let me know that on most nights she felt lonely and talked in an honest, conversational tone with God before drifting off to sleep. Clearly, Jennifer was smart and complicated, yet she had trouble following through even on the projects and class assignments she found interesting or useful.

During our counseling sessions we talked about many things that were making it hard for Jennifer to concentrate and be productive. In addition to our counseling, I offered her the chance to experiment with the "Netilat Yadayim" prayer, especially on an interesting current assignment for which she was procrastinating.

Jennifer said she would try it out, but only if she could say the prayer in her own words. Here's the version she came up with over several weeks. It's the kind of uncensored, heartfelt prayer that Jewish scholars and teachers for centuries have urged us to pray when we talk with God.

Specifically, when Jennifer got up from her desk after an hour of not getting much work done, she went to the washroom, took a deep breath, let her hands soak under the running water, and said:

Dear Invisible One.
I'm trying to talk to You.
I can feel Your silent energy at times.
But I can't seem to put a name on You or see what You look like.

Please. Please. Please shake me up right now.

Please don't let me slip into a fog.

I'm sitting at my desk like a complete slug, and my life is
    passing me by.

I need Your help to lift me out of this rut.

I know there are things, passionate things, that You've given
    me to do.

So please lift me out of my stubborn habits and self-
    destructiveness.

I've got a life to live.

I want to make a mark on this world.

Please help me be useful in ways I don't even know about yet.

I try to be tough, but I'll admit I need Your strength and Your
    love.

Please don't let me forget about You.

If I feel Your guiding presence, I'll be able to stay focused.

If I know You are with me, I'll find a way to make things
    happen in this world.

Amen.

Noticing the Changes

Does it work to say a prayer like this when you're feeling
stuck or unmotivated? In Jennifer's case the results were
extremely positive. While she continued to struggle at times
with family tensions and occasional difficulties at school,

her attitude and her life changed dramatically once she began to take control of her distractibility. As she told me during her final counseling session a few months later, "I still have moments when I put on an attitude and act like I don't give a crap. But lately those moments are rare, because most of the time I'm passionately involved in doing productive things and seeking out healthy situations. My mom is shocked at how much I've changed from being a whining slacker into someone who now actually enjoys being alive. So lately my mom complains that I'm getting involved in *too many* causes and activities. But hey, she's got to complain about something."

I can't prove the changes in Jennifer's life occurred because of the things we spoke about in counseling, or because of the natural process of maturation, or if the prayers she used truly helped her improve her focus each day. But I can say that Jennifer's use of the "Netilat Yadayim" ritual helped to bring out the very best in her, and this helped her become a real blessing to her family and her community.

I hope the same will happen for you and the people you care about who utilize this ancient prayer. For if we each find a way to raise up our actions and be of service in large and small ways, this world will be a much better place. Then, like Jennifer, we will get better at overcoming procrastination and becoming valuable blessings to those whose lives we touch each day.

CHAPTER THREE

A Prayer to Resolve Tension and Misunderstandings Between You and Someone Else

Yiva-rekh-ikha Adonai v'yish-mi-rekha	May the One bless you and safeguard you.
Ya-eir Adonai pahnahv Eilekha vikhoo-nekha	May the One illuminate your way and be gracious unto you.
Yisah Adonai pahnahv Eilekha v'yaseim likha shalom.	May the One raise up in your direction to encourage you and give you a sense of wholeness and peace.

One of the greatest joys in life is when you feel connected and in sync with someone you care about deeply. By contrast, one of the saddest moments in life is when you feel completely at odds with someone close to you, who refuses to compromise over a clash that is driving a wedge between you.

While I disagree with Sigmund Freud on some of his theories, one of his most accurate and profound teachings is that *all of our deepest relationships contain a mixture of love and exasperation.* Stop for a moment and think about your own most intimate connections—with your significant other, with your children, with a parent, or with a sibling or close friend. Haven't there been times when you and this person got on each other's nerves? Haven't there been instances when this person was so stubborn or irritating that you wondered, "How can I possibly feel so much love one moment and so much frustration the next?"

This chapter offers the Birkhat Kohanim (Priestly Blessing) as a spiritual approach for handling situations when someone close to your heart angers or saddens you. But first, recall the most recent clash or misunderstanding you had with a person who is important in your life. Perhaps you felt criticized or ignored by someone you care about. Maybe it was a serious disagreement or a painful disappointment. Or possibly it was a power struggle or a frustrating conversation between you and a family member or friend whom you love a lot but who drives you crazy at times.

Can you remember what it felt like to be in the middle of that disagreement or misunderstanding? Did you begin to feel impatient or shut off toward this person who has such an important role in your life? Did you find yourself secretly wishing this person would just go away and stop upsetting you? Did you experience hopelessness that no matter what you say to this person, there doesn't seem to be any change for the better?

As a psychologist who frequently counsels couples and families, I searched for many years for a technique to help people improve these painful situations. Especially at the moments when you say to yourself, "I've had it—this person is so frustrating to deal with," there needs to be a method for helping you regain your clarity of mind and your ability to resolve the tension and misunderstandings.

Almost thirteen years ago I happened to come across a remarkably effective technique that can help improve even the most painful disagreements and power struggles. This technique has been used for many centuries in a slightly different context as part of Jewish spiritual practice. In fact, you probably will recognize these ancient words when you hear them. Here's what happened.

Restoring the Feelings of Openness

It was 1988, and my wife, Linda, and I were invited to a friend's home for Friday night dinner. The evening started out quite hectic. The husband and wife who were hosting the dinner had been arguing. Their two-year-old child was screaming on the floor. The main course was overcooked and starting to smoke up the kitchen. A magazine salesman rang the doorbell—he must have thought that "No thank you, we're busy right now" was an invitation to sell even harder. The tension was palpable, with no sign that it was going to get better any time soon.

A few minutes later the wife lit the Sabbath candles, and the husband said a blessing over their young daughter. During these blessings I noticed the tensions and chaos dramatically lift. I remember especially the face of each person relaxing and opening up as this friend, with his hands gently reaching out over his beautiful daughter's head, repeated the ancient words "May God bless you and keep you. May God's countenance shine upon you and be gracious unto you. May God lift up God's countenance upon you and grant you peace."

It was quite amazing to see how a blessing could cut through the tension and anger that had filled the room. I began to wonder if this ancient prayer could help couples and families right at the moments when they are most upset with each other. Could these sacred words help us to remember the deeper soul connection we have to the person who is getting on our nerves? Could these words of blessing help us break out of our anger and estrangement so we might work through our differences in a healthier manner?

Eight years ago I was studying with a fascinating teacher from the Chasidic tradition (the movement founded in the eighteenth century by the Baal Shem Tov, the Master of the Good Name, who reemphasized the inherent joy and hidden mystical teachings of Judaism). This teacher spoke to me about the remarkable inner changes that take place when we stop right in the middle of an angry or sad moment to say a blessing. He suggested that if one or both people in an argument had the presence of mind to bless the other person's soul, the tensions and misunderstandings would be much easier to resolve.

That's when I began experimenting with this ancient blessing as a vehicle for helping people regain their clarity of mind and their openness to constructive ideas during a disagreement. I have seen numerous men and women use this blessing to dramatically improve how they dealt with even the most difficult family members, long-term partners, friends, and work associates. You will be surprised at how these words can open you up to a healthier way of resolving conflict.

Here are some examples of when you can use this ancient blessing (said silently in your own mind to help you regain your calmness and clarity in a tense moment):

1. If you are in an argument with a spouse or lover, instead of escalating the battle with angry or defensive words, take a moment to breathe slowly in and out as you imagine yourself blessing this person's soul with the three-part Birkhat Kohanim (Priestly Blessing).

2. If you are becoming irritated or worn out by one of your children, stop and say this ancient blessing to see if it revives your patience and your creativity.

3. If you are having a recurring dispute with a difficult parent, brother, sister, or close friend, these words can help you stop getting worked up by this person's annoying traits and regain your connection to his or her deeper essence or soul.

4. If you are in a disagreement with someone at work or in a social situation, take a moment to silently bless this person and see if it helps you become better able to navigate the situation.

5. If you want to give feedback to someone you live with or work with who has an irritating habit or a serious lack of consideration, it helps tremendously to say this prayer first to take the sting out of your criticism and help your suggestions be received more successfully.

Please note that in each of these examples the intention is not to become passive or to let the other person walk all over you. Saying a silent blessing in your own mind to help you reconnect with this person's soul or higher self is a way of rising above the conflict to a clearer perspective on the situation. By defusing the tensions inside your being, you allow yourself to break free from the adrenaline rush caused by the "fight-or-flight" human emotions that usually churn at moments like these. By saying a silent blessing, you can reconnect with your most reasonable and nondefensive self, the part of you that can come up with solutions that might work for each point of view.

"He Knows Exactly How to Tune Me Out"

As an example of how this blessing can improve your family and personal relationships, consider the situation of Rosalind, a dynamic and witty fifty-four-year-old woman who came for counseling to work on her strained relationship with her twenty-eight-year-old son, Brian. According to Rosalind, "I've always cared deeply about my son. He's my only child, and I've hung in there through each of the ups and downs of his life. But whenever we talk on the phone or see each other in person, Brian knows exactly how to tune me out. In fact, he has the same charming way of dismissing me and cutting me off that his dear old father had during the years before we got divorced. I don't want to be estranged from Brian like I am from his father. But I can't seem to change the tension I feel in my kishkas (guts) when I try to explain something to Brian and he simply goes cold and shuts me out."

In our counseling sessions it became clear that Rosalind was an excellent communicator with almost everyone in her life except her ex-husband and her son. I asked her, "Can you describe exactly what happens when you're talking with Brian that seems to trigger him putting up that wall of his?"

Rosalind thought for a moment and said, "I think I probably have an edge in my voice when I'm trying to give him suggestions or ask him about his problems at work or with his most recent relationship. When I first start talking to Brian on the phone, my voice is calm, but as soon as I sense he's tuning me out I start talking a little faster, a little louder, and a little more desperately . . . which I'm sure causes his wall to go up each time."

As in most family conflicts, both sides were contributing to the miscommunication. Rosalind knew the only thing she could control was her own behavior—the edginess in her voice and the irritation she felt because of how much her son's tuning her out reminded her of her ex-husband. So we began to explore creative ways of improving Rosalind's side of the communication. We talked about her painful memories of being dismissed and belittled by her ex. We dug deeply into how frustrating it was to long for a connection with Brian but then to find he was almost as impatient and dismissive as his father had been.

In addition, we began to experiment with using the three-sentence Priestly Blessing as a way to improve Rosalind's frame of mind and tone of voice whenever she was beginning to feel tense in a conversation with her son. It took several attempts before Rosalind felt comfortable saying these words during the exact moments when Brian was putting up his wall. At first, Rosalind found, "I didn't feel much like blessing my son when he was being such a pain." But over the next few weeks Rosalind began to say the blessings silently in her head whenever she felt a conflict with Brian. During their twice-weekly phone calls and occasional visits, she calmly said the ancient words to herself as she thought about how deeply she longed for a better way of connecting with her only child.

A few weeks later she told me, "I had a bit of a break-through with Brian. We were having a phone call last night about his wanting to borrow more money from me. At first I started to feel the same frustration and tension I'd often felt with him. But then I remembered to say the three blessings silently in my mind. Within a few moments I was feeling a lot more open and relaxed. To my surprise, we had one of our best talks ever, a nondefensive conversation about what's really going on with his career and what might be some ways for him to get his cash flow going again. Even though I had to say no to lending him more money, the tone of our talk was so loving and supportive that before he got off the phone, Brian said to me what he almost never says any longer. He said, 'I love you, Mom, and I appreciate how you try to do what's right for me.'"

Over the next several months Rosalind and Brian continued to improve their ability to talk about what really mattered in each other's lives. As Rosalind commented, "Brian still has some irritating habits that do remind me of his dear old dad. But now I can stop myself from overreacting because

I take a moment silently to say these blessings. As a result, I'm much better at staying calm and finding the right words when we're talking on the phone or we see each other in person. I do love my son, and I want God to watch over him and protect him. So now when I say the ancient words of blessing, it's more than just a way of cooling myself down. It's a way of reconnecting with that precious soul, my only child, whom I will always love."

What the Words Mean on a Deeper Level

You probably have heard many times this traditional blessing, "May God bless you and keep you . . ." Many rabbis say these words lovingly when they bless the congregation at Sabbath and High Holiday services, as well as at weddings, baby namings, circumcisions, bar and bat mitzvah ceremonies, and other events. If you've ever been in certain traditional synagogues you may have seen the Kohanim (those congregants whose ancestry traces back to the priestly members of the Hebrew tribe) come forward with their prayer shawls over their heads to ask God to distribute these ancient blessings to the participants. Many Christian services also include these traditional Jewish phrases as a standard way of blessing someone.

This three-sentence Birkhat Kohanim (Priestly Blessing) goes as far back as the biblical description of Moses and his brother Aaron in the Sinai wilderness. In the fourth book of the Torah, the Book of Numbers (6:22–27), Moses receives an instruction from God to teach Aaron the priest and all future generations how to be vehicles, conduits for requesting God's blessings for each of the gathered multitude. The biblical description says in essence that if you want God's loving energy to make an impact on someone, these are the three sentences that can help make that happen. Now, what do the words actually mean?

Blessing 1:
May the One bless you and safeguard you.

The first three Hebrew words, *"Yiva-rekh-ikha Adonai v'yish-mi-rekha,"* often get translated "May God bless you and keep you." Other scholars have translated them more literally as "May God bless you and safeguard you" or "May God bless you and protect you," since the word *v'yish-mi-rekha* contains the root *shomeir,* which means "one who watches over, protects, or safeguards something special." For example, you may have heard the term *shomeir Shabbat,* which refers to those people who guard the traditions and true purposes of the Sabbath; in many congregations there is a volunteer or paid individual called the *shomeir,* who has a special responsibility to guard and protect the vision and true purpose of the community he or she serves.

So when you ask for divine assistance in guarding or protecting someone, you are essentially asking God to help this individual live up to his or her true purpose. This interpretation corresponds to the teachings of a nineteenth-century scholar named Naphtali Zevi Judah Berlin (nicknamed ha-Neziv). He was the head of the Yeshiva (religious school) at Volozhin in Russia and the spiritual leader for Russian Jewry for forty years. In his widely read commentaries on the Torah, ha-Neziv wrote that *"Yiva-rekh-ikha Adonai v'yish-mi-rekha* implies how God gives a specific blessing appropriate to each person according to that person's particular needs and qualities—the student will be blessed with learning and the merchant with good business, etc. Only if you know the soul or essence of a person can you begin to understand the way that God's love flows through that individual."

Ha-Neziv continues, *"Yish-mi-rekha* (to safeguard) means that this blessing must be guarded so that it would not, God forbid, be turned to a wrong purpose. The Torah scholar requires guardianship to save him from pride and bringing the name of the Lord into disrepute, and the like. The businessman requires guardianship against his wealth becoming a stumbling block to him as in the case of those who lost their way spiritually because of their material success."

Because this first blessing asks the Eternal One to help the person in question fulfill his or her unique purpose and to be safeguarded against misusing those gifts, I tend to favor the translation "May the One bless you and safeguard you." It has both the wish for your family member or friend to do well and the realistic caution that this person will need guidance to stay on track.

Blessing 2:
May the One illuminate your way and be gracious unto you.

The second Hebrew phrase, consisting of five words, *"Ya-eir Adonai pahnahv Eilekha vikhoo-nekha,"* usually gets translated, "May God's face or countenance shine upon you and be gracious unto you." According to the standard interpretation, if the Divine Presence turns away from you, it means God is angry at you, but if God's face (a metaphor, because God does not have a corporeal body) shines upon you, it's like a smile that lights up with favor and support.

A different way of looking at this blessing comes from Rabbi Ovadiah of Sforno, Italy, who wrote classic Torah commentaries in the fifteenth century. The Sforno interpretation states that you are asking God to illuminate or enlighten this person so that he or she will be able to use the gifts given in the first blessing with wisdom. Specifically, Sforno writes, "Having received God's blessing, we then need the peace of mind to go beyond the elementary requirements of survival to a deeper enlightenment about our role in God's intricate creation."

So I recommend translating the second line as "May the One illuminate your way and be gracious unto you," because it asks for the person being blessed to see more clearly and act more gracefully on a continuing basis. Many people associate God with light, both the light of creation and the inner light of wisdom and compassion. The word *ya-eir* in this blessing literally means "God's light." So this Hebrew phrase asks that the person you are trying to bless might somehow open up to the energies of light that can help him or her navigate in life with more grace. Wouldn't that be a blessing—if the person who currently is upsetting you were to open up and be illuminated by a loving Presence that can guide him or her to act more graciously! As you say the second sentence of this prayer, let that be your hope.

Blessing 3:
May the One raise up in your direction to encourage
you and give you a sense of wholeness and peace.

The third blessing, consisting of seven words, "*Yisah Adonai pahnahv Eilekha v'yaseim likha shalom,*" often gets translated "May God lift up his countenance toward you and grant you peace." The usual interpretation of *yisah* (lift up) and *pahnahv Eilekha* (God's face or countenance) is that if someone lifts up her face toward you it means she approves, shows favor, or is paying attention to you. Or if someone holds his head down or turns away from you, it means he's frustrated, ashamed, or distant from you.

With regard to this blessing (and what it means for the person you are frustrated with and trying to feel good about again), there is an interesting interpretation given by a nineteenth-century scholar from Vilna, Lithuania. His name was Moreinu HaRav Zeev Wolf Einhorn (nicknamed Maharzu, based on his initials M, H, R, Z). He wrote that if God can love the people of Israel even when we make mistakes or show our weaknesses, then this blessing is a reminder that we need not inflict shame on ourselves or others for our struggles in life. Maharzu says that just as God can lift up to pay attention and look directly into our souls no matter what we do, we should pay attention and see the complexity of others' souls without requiring them to hide or bow their heads in shame.

In psychological terms, this blessing offers two opposing choices on how to deal with your own imperfections and those of the people who get on your nerves. The common choice is to see our human weaknesses as shameful and to respond with discouraging remarks, such as "You idiot," "I'm fed up with you," or "I can't stand to look at you—you should be ashamed."

The less common but more spiritual choice is to follow God's lead and lift up our energies to encourage ourselves and others, even at our most vulnerable moments. Instead of telling us to live in shame, this blessing ends in the word *shalom,* which means "peace" or "wholeness." It implies that if you want to achieve inner peace, you need to look directly at our human imperfections and not hide from them in shame. That's why, based on Maharzu's interpretation of this blessing, I favor the translation "May the One raise up in your direction to encourage you and give you a sense of wholeness and peace."

To summarize, I am offering one of many interpretive versions you can use for silently reciting the Birkhat Kohanim, the Priestly Blessing, as a way of unhooking your mind from conflict and regaining your calm and inner strength. But I urge you to utilize whatever translation you find most inspiring and comfortable. If you have a particular connection to any of the traditional ways of translating these three blessings or to an alternative that comes from your own studies or teachers, please feel free to use whatever has truth for you.

Here again is the interpretation my counseling clients and I have found extremely useful. While breathing in and out slowly, you can picture the soul or essence of the person with whom you are in conflict as you say the following words with sincerity:

Yiva-rekh-ikha Adonai v'yish-mi-rekha.
May the One bless you and safeguard you.

Ya-eir Adonai pahnahv Eilekha vikhoo-nekha.
May the One illuminate your way and be gracious unto you.

Yisah Adonai pahnahv Eilekha v'yaseim likha shalom.
May the One raise up in your direction to encourage you and give you a sense of wholeness and peace.

Amen.

The Trouble Most People Have

While these ancient words of blessing sound hopeful, you still might find that cutting through your anger or exasperation at a particular person is not easy. Here are some explanations from counseling clients and friends of why they had trouble asking God for a blessing for someone who was getting on their nerves:

"I felt strange asking God to help with someone who at that moment I was close to writing off."

"I didn't want to admit to myself just how mad I was with this individual, so talking to God about it was quite uncomfortable because usually I try to hide from God when I'm angry or upset."

"I was afraid that if I asked God to bless this stubborn creep and the blessings helped him be even more successful, then I was helping the wrong person. I'm the one who needs a boost here, so why should I ask for this other person to be blessed?"

"I simply didn't want to let go of my anger. Yet I knew that if I really thought about this person's soul and I asked God to bless her, I would have to lighten up and be friendly again, which I wasn't ready to do just yet."

As you experiment with this technique for changing the tone of an argument or dispute, you might find yourself having similar hesitations. It's quite normal to want to hold on to what feels like justified anger and resentment. In fact, it might even feel threatening and somewhat uncomfortable to be considering this other person's soul or essence in the middle of a heated conflict. But I assure you that if you do manage to rise above the tension long enough to connect with the divine sparks hidden deep within this individual, or if you take a moment to ask that this person's soul be blessed, you will start to notice a dramatic shift in your mental clarity and your access to productive solutions.

What most people fear is that they are going to be mistreated or victimized if they let go of their anger and resentment. But if you think about it you'll realize that your feelings of anger and frustration are already victimizing you. Wouldn't it be more empowering to be able to look at the situation from a spiritual perspective—that you and this other person are two souls on a journey trying to learn and grow but getting stuck from time to time in old habits and painful behaviors?

I want to reemphasize, please don't think of this blessing as a type of resignation or surrender. Asking God to bless this other person's soul doesn't mean you have to put up with additional mistreatment or emotional abuse. Nor does it mean you are supposed to "kiss and make up" in a forced or insincere way.

Rather this technique of silently saying a blessing is *the first step toward beginning a healthy, nondefensive dialogue about how the two of you can improve your relationship.* Instead of snapping at the other person or stuffing your frustration inside, with this blessing you can gain the calmness and clarity to start working constructively toward a peaceful resolution. It is the beginning of a sensible, creative course of action.

Giving Rebuke with Love

In Jewish tradition there are numerous teachings about how to confront irritating behaviors and make an impact on the person by using compassion and decency. Some scholars call this "giving rebuke with integrity." Others call it "giving rebuke with love." If you learn how this remarkable process works, you will no longer get trapped in resentment or victimization when you are in a conflict with someone. Instead you will have a greater ability to offer ideas for improving your key relationships without saying something that will make matters worse.

What exactly does it mean to give rebuke with love? Let's face it—most of us are not accustomed to giving feedback in a calm or caring way, especially with family members, friends, or lovers, who tend to upset us the most. In fact, many people automatically assume that confrontation or giving rebuke has to be rough or harsh. This misunderstanding is so widespread that in the new Microsoft *Encarta Dictionary* the word *rebuke* is defined this way: "to tell off, to criticize or reprimand somebody, usually sharply."

Yet if you study the word *rebuke* in most Jewish sources and spiritual writings, you will find it has a much different tone. From ancient and modern Jewish teachings you will discover specific ways to stand up for yourself with a difficult person without making the situation worse. Here are a few of the key Jewish teachings on giving rebuke with integrity and compassion. You can use them immediately after your willingness to say the Birkhat Kohanim (the Priestly Blessing) silently toward the person who is irritating you.

The first principle cited in several Jewish writings is to make sure that you never rebuke or criticize someone to the point of embarrassment. According to the great twelfth-century scholar Moses ben Maimon (often referred to as Maimonides), this means to carry out your conversation in private and in a way that shows respect for the overall good character and soul of the person about whose behavior you are commenting. Your carefully chosen words and nonverbal actions must convey compassion for the individual's essence while at the same time asking him or her to reexamine the specific behavior that is causing you discomfort.

The second principle is that you must make sure you aren't trying to blast someone else for what you yourself need to be working on. The biblical Book of Zephaniah (2:2) says: "Remove the chaff from yourself, then remove it from others." Almost two thousand years ago in the Babylonian Talmud (a key commentary on Jewish law and teachings), Rabbi Nathan said: "Reproach not your neighbor for a blemish that is yours."

If you do decide to bring up to someone a bad habit or quality that you share, it's more helpful to work as nonjudgmental allies than for you to act in an accusatory or self-righteous manner toward this person who's exhibiting the very same trait you struggle with. For example, if you want to criticize a loved one for not listening well to you, take a moment first to see how well you've been listening to this person. If you recognize that you, too, need some work on your ability to listen patiently without jumping in to fix or criticize, then you should admit up front that you both need to work on this issue. Instead of saying or implying, "You have the problem and I don't," it's far more constructive to say, "We've both hurt each other by not listening as well as we could. We're both going to need to work hard on this so we don't keep frustrating each other."

The third principle is to make sure you carry out your feedback or suggestions with such delicacy that the other person feels supported and loved by your comments rather than bruised or picked on. This "delicacy" is so hard to achieve that a widely respected second-century scholar, Rabbi Akiva, remarked: "I wonder whether there is anyone in this generation who knows how to give reproof without humiliating the one reproved."

The next time you're ready to comment on the behavior of someone you live with, work with, or are related to, ask yourself whether you feel sure that you're not going to embarrass the other person, that you're not projecting your own struggles onto him or her, and that you are calm enough to speak with the utmost delicacy and love. Only after you have said a blessing for the other person's soul and you're feeling relaxed enough to treat this human being with respect and patience are you ready to engage in a healthy dialogue.

There is no guarantee that your feedback will be accepted immediately. But by offering your carefully timed and calmly worded rebuke with love, you greatly increase the likelihood that the other person will hear and consider your point of view. I have found that when men and women stop in the middle of a dispute to say the Priestly Blessing and abide by the spiritual principles of healthy rebuke giving, they usually either make some progress in improving the relationship or, even if the other person doesn't change very much, at least feel good about having spoken with integrity and clarity.

"I Know How to Control My Temper When I'm at Work"

Donald and Shelly's case is a good illustration of the importance of saying the Priestly Blessing and utilizing the Jewish teachings on giving rebuke with love. A married couple in their thirties, Donald and Shelly came in for counseling almost a year ago.

Donald, an engineer with a telecommunications company, was hoping the sessions would make Shelly "less moody and overreactive." As he explained, "Whenever I say something to Shelly—about the mess in the kids' bedrooms or about her forgetting to get a second bid on the remodeling of our kitchen—she gets all bent out of shape and goes into a funk that can last for hours or even days."

Shelly, a technical writer who works from home, had a different goal for the counseling. She said, "The biggest problem in our marriage is that Donald is a perfectionist and a rage-aholic. He can be extremely loving and supportive, but every so often he blows up about some innocent mistake or miscommunication. He unleashes this quick flood of verbal abuse, and then he seems to feel a sense of relief from having vented his anger. Meanwhile, I'm still reeling from the 'I could kill you' expression on his face and his sarcastic, somewhat vicious way of pointing out my imperfections. Quite often he blows up at me in front of our kids or in front of friends or relatives at a dinner party or a family event. Our kids are only two and six, but I can see already that they're scared of their father's anger, and they seem very agitated by the fights they see us have."

As I explained to Donald and Shelly, my job as a therapist would not be to take sides or be a judge. Rather, it would be to help them find a healthier way of working through their tensions and misunderstandings. So I began by asking Shelly, "What would you like Donald to do when he notices he's getting upset inside about something he thinks isn't being handled right? What specific way of talking about his frustrations and needs would feel okay to you and not leave you reeling in pain or apprehension?"

Shelly thought about the type of feedback she preferred, and she suggested, "I grew up with a mom who was loving and caring one moment but then upset and harshly critical the next moment. I think if I just had the sense that Donald cares about me as a person and that he's not seeing me as incompetent or negligent, it would be much easier to hear what's on his mind. I don't want to keep slipping into a funk every time Donald is frustrated with something I did imperfectly. But it's such an old pattern with me—to be criticized brutally and then to withdraw into myself."

Donald responded angrily, "See, there you go again. You're always assuming that I don't love you or that I'm some sort of angry monster. I do care about you, but I have a right to be upset because of the out-to-lunch way you handle things."

When we began to explore Donald's side of the problem—his short fuse and feelings of righteous indignation—some interesting information was revealed. I asked him, "When mistakes are made at work, what kind of tone do you use for giving feedback?" Donald thought for a moment and admitted, "That's different. I know how to control my temper when I'm at work. In fact, my bosses and my key customer think I'm a helluva nice guy."

Donald and Shelly were like many men and women who know how to communicate effectively in one setting but tend to fall back into old habits at home or with loved ones. For the next several sessions we discussed and tried out the two steps described in this chapter: saying the blessings to regain your clarity of mind when you are upset with your partner; and practicing the delicate art of giving rebuke with love.

At first Shelly was hesitant. She explained, "I just don't feel like offering a blessing to Donald right at the moment when he slimes me with his self-righteous anger." But over the next few weeks she began to give it a try. She reported, "It's strange how when I say these ancient words I seem to regain a sense of strength and a connection to who I am that's bigger than just being a scolded child with my volatile mom or a scolded wife with my perfectionist husband. I quickly arrive at a place where I feel healthy and alive again. I begin to see Donald as a wounded soul who deeply longs to have order in his world, and I don't take it so personally when he's upset because his world just won't abide by the orderliness he craves."

Donald's response to these two spiritual steps was somewhat different. He told us at a later session, "I think in the past I had wanted to toughen Shelly up, and that's why I would berate her with such intensity. I got yelled at quite often as a kid, and I felt as though it made me a tougher and more successful person." He continued, "But now I realize that my sarcasm and my angry explosions are having the opposite effect. There was an argument two weeks ago between Shelly and me with the kids in the room. I said my piece, and I felt extremely justified in being angry. But then I looked over and saw the fear in Shelly's eyes and the sadness in our elder daughter's face. I don't want to alienate these people I love, and I can sense that my way of 'toughening them up' is actually pushing them away. As a result, I got serious about trying this gentler approach, and I was impressed at how well it works."

According to Donald, "What I noticed with Shelly is that when I take a moment to calm myself down by saying the blessings, she can listen much better to what I'm upset about. And if I talk to her in the most respectful way I can muster, she's a much more responsive and competent partner. We've handled several situations in the past few weeks so much more quickly and successfully since I started using a tone that she can hear. It's made things a lot less stressful and tense at home, which we both have needed ever since the kids came into our lives."

In Your Own Words

I'll admit that the assignment in this chapter is not an easy one. To stop in the middle of a dispute and silently request a blessing on the very person who is upsetting you—maybe that's asking for too much. But if you want to find a way to resolve the basic dilemma of every intense emotional relationship—how to treat each other with love and respect even when you are in a battle over who's right—this approach can make a huge difference.

For some people saying the English and/or the Hebrew words of blessing silently can turn things around. For many others it helps to add personalized words. As an example, here are the exact words that Shelly and Donald used in addition to the ancient blessings.

Shelly recalls saying silently,

Dear God, I know that I love my husband, Donald, even though right now I've completely lost sight of what is lovable about him. He's so self-righteous and preachy sometimes. I need Your help, God. I need You to bless this man with light and a gracefulness that I've seen Donald have at other times. I need Your Presence to watch over and guide him so that he doesn't cause me to lose my hope for this marriage. Please, God, bless him with the ability to see that there are two sides to this argument and that both of us have some wisdom to offer. Please, God, bless us as parents to be smart enough to work through our disagreements in a more loving way.

Donald said that he was making an effort whenever he felt angry with Shelly to stop, take a deep breath, and say silently the traditional blessings or a prayer in his own words. Here is one example of the words he used to calm himself down:

Dear God, whatever You are and wherever You might be, help me right now to find the love and respect I know in my heart I feel for Shelly. Please bless Shelly and the kids with Your light and Your protection. Help me to control my anger and not to say or do anything that will make this argument be longer or more painful than it already is. Please help me to shut up and let Shelly have a turn so we can work this thing out like grown-ups. And please don't let me push her or the kids away with my verbal daggers or my angry scowl. I need some of Your strength, God, to get control of my anger. I need Your love to make me a more loving and patient human being.

According to both Shelly and Donald, the prayer was successful. Instead of unloading his anger on his wife, Donald was able to initiate a healthy conversation in which both of them felt heard and respected.

All of us have moments when we feel self-righteous and angry. Those are the moments when we tend to forget that the other person has a soul and a vulnerable, sensitive interior. Those are the moments when regrettable things get said and when painful hurts begin to drive a wedge between us and someone we care about. Will it help to stop and ask for a blessing to be given to the person with whom you are quarreling? I certainly hope so. Especially if you care about this relationship, take a moment to ask for help from the mysterious Source that is bigger than the two of you. Even if the other person continues to be difficult, at least you will have regained your inner peace and your highest effectiveness.

CHAPTER FOUR

A Prayer So You Can Unwind and Find Peace at Least Three Times a Day

Barookh Atah Adonai	Blessed are You, Eternal One,
Eloheinu melekh ha-olam	Energy Source of the universe,
ha-motzi lekhem min ha-aretz	Who brings forth bread from the earth.

(OR)

Barookh Atah Adonai	Blessed are You, Eternal One,
Eloheinu melekh ha-olam	Energy Source of the universe,
sheh-hakol nih-hiyeh bid-varo.	Through Whose expression Everything came to be.

Think about it for a moment—we human beings eat a huge number of meals. For most people there are 365 dinners and nearly as many lunches and breakfasts each year. With the average life expectancy over seventy years, that means you will probably eat more than 25,000 dinners, 25,000 lunches, and many thousands of breakfasts during your time on Earth.

Now ask yourself this question: During how many of these meals do you take a moment to consider the extraordinary way food comes into being and how a meal nourishes us for living our lives? How often do you think about what might be the source and the steps by which food reaches your fingertips? Have you ever stopped to consider what it means to be alive in a body that can enjoy the smell, the taste, the good company, and the life-sustaining properties of a delicious meal? Or, like most people, do you just chow down hurriedly with your mind on something else?

This chapter will say some unusual and thought-provoking things about the connection between food and spirituality. If you carefully explore these ideas, you might be amazed at how they can affect your physical health and spiritual clarity. In addition, if you have ever had a problem with food—weight problems, dieting frustrations, digestion difficulties, ulcers, sluggishness, hunger cravings, or hypoglycemia—this chapter provides a spiritual approach for dealing with these "gut" issues. But before we explore any sacred teachings, let's look realistically at how you and your family or friends tend to eat a meal.

What Comes with the Meal?

What do you remember about the way you related to food and family meals when you were a child? Was the dinner table a calm and loving place? Or was it filled with tension, power struggles, or frequent interruptions from the phone or television? Did your family relax and feel connected each time they came together for a meal? Or were you all so busy you rarely had time to break bread together?

Now think about the past few days and weeks. Have your meals been relaxing and refreshing, or have they been rushed and stressful? When in recent days or weeks have you felt surrounded by love and warmth at a meal? When have you felt lonely from eating by yourself or at odds with certain meal companions?

Let's face it—the tension that most people bring to their meals is substantial. Sometimes we're rushing to prepare a meal quickly (possibly with kids screaming or family members complaining about how long it's taking). Sometimes we're rushing to get the meal over with because we have to get to work, to a class, to an appointment, or to a movie. We might be entering the meal feeling agitated because there's a disagreement or a long-running clash with someone who is nearby. Or we might be eating in a rush to quell our anxiety, or our stress, boredom, or unhappiness.

No matter how committed you are to a diet, a health program, or the desire to have an enjoyable meal, the time constraints and stresses you bring to the table can disrupt your best intentions. I've found that even extremely knowledgeable and health-conscious people have a habit of bombarding their digestive systems with anxious thoughts and self-imposed pressures that can sabotage the most nutritious meal.

For example, several years ago, when I was living in New York, I happened to be at the old Brownie's Health Food Restaurant on Fifth Avenue and Sixteenth Street when I saw at the next table one of the most respected health experts in the world. This man had written two best-sellers about holistic health and was renowned for his cutting-edge research on how to live longer. As I glanced in his direction during the meal, however, I noticed that this health expert was gobbling down his food. He seemed to be in a huge rush.

I went back to my own meal and tried to ignore the stressful look on this eminent man's face. But then I overheard his wife urging him to slow down. He gave her a sharp glare as if to say, "Don't tell me what to do." The couple's selection of food had been extremely healthy. But I wondered if anyone's body could have successfully digested and absorbed such an anxiously consumed meal.

A few years later I read in the newspaper that this health pioneer had died of a "sudden" heart attack. The news made me think about what I had seen at the restaurant. I know that many of our health problems are genetically based. But I wonder if we fully realize how we might be causing or worsening our heart and digestive problems by the stressful way we show up at meals. Do you ever wonder how our bodies can digest the food that gets gulped down during our time-pressured and stress-filled meals?

What You Can Do to Change a Lifelong Habit of Stressful Eating

In Jewish spiritual practice there is a subtle but extremely powerful technique for transforming your state of mind at least three times a day. This tradition of saying a blessing before eating goes back thousands of years. The Bible (I Samuel 9:13) says that the Israelites waited for food to be blessed before they would partake of it. The first-century Jewish and Roman historian Flavius Josephus described in detail the grace said before meals by the Essene sect of Jews, who lived in ancient Palestine.

In modern times most observant Jews say a prayer before meals, but if you ask them why the ritual exists, the majority will say it's just a tradition. Very few people know the spiritual significance of these blessings; in fact most modern Jews dig right into a meal without pausing. It's safe to say that more than 75 percent of contemporary Jews think of "saying grace" as an unnecessary relic, except on special occasions like a wedding, a bar or bat mitzvah, a Passover seder, or maybe when religiously observant relatives come over for a meal.

However, some people find the conscious act of unwinding before a meal and connecting with something holy and profound one of the great benefits of being a spiritual person. If you study the deeper levels of wisdom for the blessings over food, you will be surprised at how much these ancient words can affect your emotions, your health, and your soul. For example, one of the reasons to say a prayer before eating is to lift your awareness from the grumbling of your belly and focus for a moment on the beauty of being alive in a world where food is abundant and comes from a remarkable interaction of seeds, sunlight, soil, water, cultivation, and harvesting—the bountiful creation that we often forget about if we live in paved-over cities.

According to Evelyn Garfiel, a widely respected modern lecturer on Judaism and psychology who taught for many years at the Jewish Theological Seminary in Chicago and wrote *Service of the Heart: A Guide to the Jewish Prayer Book,*

"The prayer before eating is not just for offering thanks, but to remind us that even the simplest, least unusual events in life are endowed with significance—that everyday experience is lifted out of the merely routine and given a sense of holiness. We take a moment to remember the ultimate source of the food, which is God's loving care."

As you think about your own experiences when saying a prayer before eating, have there been moments when the words you said felt healing or inspiring? Have you ever felt a change inside yourself physically, emotionally, or spiritually because you took a moment to say a traditional or a spontaneous blessing over food?

I remember several years ago when a prayer my wife and I said before eating moved me to tears. Linda and I had gone through eight years of trying to start a family. We had endured two Tay-Sachs pregnancies, in which the fetuses were tested and shown to have no chance of being able to live and thrive. We had gone through several months of supporting a birth mother in Iowa and had flown there for the delivery, only to find she was unable to relinquish the child. We had cried and been frustrated time and again.

But in 1994 we became a family, and we were sitting down to one of our first meals with our son, Steven. Sure it was hectic with a kid who had an attention span of less than two seconds. And we were tired from sleepless nights and so much new activity. Yet as we looked into each other's eyes and said a blessing for the food we were about to eat, we felt connected to the mystery and the miracle of life. Our eyes filled with tears because of how much it meant to be together as a family, sharing this moment after so much waiting, disappointment, prayer, and persistence. Each time since then when the three of us join hands and say a blessing before a meal, I think back on how deep was our longing to become a family and how beautiful it is to be sharing a meal with people I love.

When I ask friends and clients for their memories of a time when the blessing before a meal meant a lot to them, most seem to have several instances come to mind. See if any of the following stir up your own recollections:

> One of my counseling clients is a Holocaust survivor who remembers the first meal she ate after she was liberated from the concentration camp. She recalls, "It felt like a miracle to hold a piece of bread in my hand and say, 'Blessed are You, Holy One, who brings forth bread from the earth."

> One of my close friends is a Roman Catholic woman who learned in her family to say a prayer of thanks before each meal for the individuals who grew the food, helped to transport it from the farm to the city, and prepared and served the food. She explains, "When I take a moment to think about all the men and women who did their part to make this nutritious food available to me, I feel connected to God and how God's love flows through a chain of human kindness and reaches us in mysterious ways."

> A therapy client of mine who has successfully overcome a serious eating disorder told me recently, "When I stop

before a meal and take a deep breath to feel thankful for the nutritious food I'm about to eat, my body starts to relax a bit. That moment of quieting my mind and slowing myself down helps me to eat in a calmer and less anxious way, which in my case makes a huge difference in keeping me from overeating."

A rabbi friend told me recently that the reason he loves the blessing before a meal is because it snaps him out of the rushing, giving, achieving activities of his day and opens him up to the receiving, relaxing, grateful part of life. He says, "Even though serving as a rabbi means being on call and responding to so many different demands on my time, I still have at least three chances a day to recharge my energy and feel the inflow of loving energy from a mysterious Source. And if I have a couple of snacks each day and say a prayer then, too, I can have five times a day to stop rushing and feel at peace for at least a moment."

A psychologist friend of mine explains, "I didn't grow up saying prayers or blessings. They seemed old-fashioned and somewhat servantlike, thanking the master for every little thing. But in recent years I've begun to realize that I truly could not survive if it weren't for how the universe has been mysteriously set up with so many different foods that are produced in such abundance. Each time I sit down to a meal, I try to spend at least a few seconds wondering what kind of God or creative force would be so brilliant to have sparked so many delicious ways of

satisfying our hunger. After a few moments of appreciating the richness of creation and saying a prayer of
thanks, I usually find the food tastes better than if I just
started chomping down my meal while obsessing about
whatever worries are pressing that day."

A busy two-career couple I counseled recently said they
wanted their three young children to grow up with a
stronger sense of spirituality and centeredness. I asked
them if they would try for a few weeks stopping before
every family meal to let each child and adult thank God or
the universe for something that meant a lot to that person.
The couple told me four weeks later, "Our kids resisted
the first night, but when they saw we really cared and we
wanted to know what they were thankful for, they began
to enjoy this mealtime ritual. All of our three children
seem to relish having a turn to speak up and announce
something for which they are thankful. These blessings
before each family meal have changed the tone of our
dinners from what used to be complaints and power
struggles to some wonderful sharing of what's going right
in each of our different, busy lives. Our family time *does*
feel a lot more spiritual and centered as a result."

Choosing Which Words Give
You the Strongest Connection

Regardless of whether you grew up with a certain way of
blessing a meal or with no such experience, please take a

moment to consider the several possibilities recommended in Jewish spiritual traditions. Most Jews think of the prayer before a meal as the *motzi,* the traditional prayer over bread that says, *"Barookh Atah Adonai Eloheinu melekh ha-olam, ha-motzi lekhem min ha-aretz,"* which can be translated as "Blessed are You, Eternal One, Energy Source of the universe, who brings forth bread from the earth."

In Jewish tradition bread is considered the "staff of life," and if a meal has any bread in it, this *"ha-motzi lekhem min ha-aretz"* (thanks to the One who brings forth bread from the earth) can serve as the prayer of thanks for the entire meal. Some people like to hold up the bread during the blessing and connect with the smell and touch of this loaf that comes from fields of grain stalks blowing in the wind and being nourished by sunlight and showers. Others prefer to hold hands with their loved ones while saying these ancient words and connecting with the warmth and companionship that make a meal more than just the consuming of food.

In addition, Jewish spiritual practice has a specific way of helping us connect with the holiness of the moment. If there is no bread served at the meal, the tradition asks us to look closely at the food and see it not just as something to eat but as something that comes from somewhere else—to notice that it has a history and an origin. That's why if there is no bread in the meal for a *motzi* prayer, Jewish tradition says to consider the specific source of the nourishment:

Is it fruit from a tree? If so, the prayer is *"Barookh Atah Adonai Eloheinu melekh ha-olam, borei p'ri ha-eitz,"* which can be translated, "Blessed are You, Eternal One, guiding force of the universe, who creates the fruit of the tree."

Is it something that grows directly from the earth? If so, the blessing is *"Barookh Atah Adonai Eloheinu melekh ha-olam, borei p'ri ha-adamah,"* or in English, "Blessed are You, Eternal One, guiding force of the universe, who creates the fruit of the ground."

Is it a grain such as wheat, barley, rye, oats, spelt, or (according to many opinions) rice? If so, the prayer is *"Barookh Atah Adonai Eloheinu melekh ha-olam, borei mi-nei m'zohnoht,"* which is translated, "Blessed are You, Eternal One, guiding force of the universe, who creates species of nourishment."

Is it grape wine or grape juice? If so, the blessing is *"Barookh Atah Adonai Eloheinu melekh ha-olam, borei p'ri hagafen,"* or "Blessed are You, Eternal One, guiding force of the universe, who creates the fruit of the vine."

Stopping to think about the way this food came into being draws you closer to the ultimate source—the Creator of the universe—whose wisdom is in the cells, the genetic code, the nutritional content of every type of food. Whenever I remember to consider the origin of the various foods on my plate, I usually feel a sense of awe that we human beings are part of an infinite web of creation. It's humbling to think about the vast universe we live in, and the thought usually causes me to take a breath and slow down.

The All-Encompassing Prayer for Food

Jewish tradition says that if you're not sure how the food came into being or if you want to say an all-encompassing prayer, the preferred blessing is *"Barookh Atah Adonai Eloheinu melekh ha-olam, sheh-hakol nih-hih-yeh bid-varo,"* which translates as "Blessed are You, Eternal One, Energy Source of the universe, through Whose word or expression everything came to be."

I find this a very inspiring prayer because if you search deeply for the meaning of the phrase "through Whose word or expression everything came to be," you will uncover one of the more mystical and important ideas about how God is viewed in Jewish spirituality. Let me describe a widely accepted interpretation of this phrase, which I hope will stimulate your own ideas about the mysterious nature of the Divine Presence.

First, a note about the difference between what you learned about God as a child and what you will find if you study Jewish spirituality as an adult. Most of us grew up in families and religious schools where God was portrayed as an old man with white hair above the clouds throwing thunderbolts to get things going. Some people carry that image into adulthood, and many say they believe in God or they can't believe in God based only on that white-haired anthropomorphic image.

But in many Jewish teachings, especially the Kabbalistic writings, there is a very different idea of God, as an energy force, a thought pattern, an unfolding process. This force or pattern has desire and intention, which get expressed or re-vealed in the world. This ongoing creative process of making a world and improving the world is itself God.

As Rabbi David Cooper describes in his book *God Is a Verb*, we can understand the divine energies better if we think of God as an active force, a verb, rather than as a static thing, a noun. Rabbi Cooper writes, "God is not what we think It is. God is not a thing, a being, a noun. It does not exist, as existence is usually defined, for It takes up no space and is not bound by time. Jewish mystics often refer to It as Ein Sof, which means Endlessness. Mystics teach that there is a universal connection among all things; modern science offers the same message. This connection has various names. Some say it is a soul force, others call it love; the ancients called it ether, science often names it energy. In Judaism this Ein Sof is not the name of a thing, but is an ongoing process."

This idea of God as an ongoing process that has no restric-tive name corresponds to the moment in the Book of Exodus (3:13–14) when Moses says to God, "When I come to the Israelites and they ask me, 'What is the Name of the God who has sent me to you,'—what shall I say to them?" The answer you'll find in Exodus 3:14 is a mysterious *"Eh-hih-yeh asheyr eh-hih-yeh,"* which can be translated as "I am becoming what I am becoming." In other words, God probably is not a nar-rowly defined "thing" but rather a hard-to-define continual process of becoming.

In the Jewish mystical tradition this active force that we call God is forever expressing itself in the world. So when the Book of Genesis says, "God spoke and there was light" or "God spoke and the seas were formed," it probably doesn't mean an old man with white hair spoke. Rather it means that God's word or God's expression is revealed in the creation we see all around us. This active and eternal energy force is continually speaking and expressing, so we say, "through Whose word or expression everything came to be."

This idea of God as an expressive, creative force is described beautifully by Rabbi Marcia Prager of Philadelphia in her book *The Path of Blessing*. She writes, "For centuries Jewish mystics and kabbalists have explored the earliest stories of Torah for clues about the origin of the universe and the mystery we call Creation. From their teachings we discern that God's speaking Creation into existence must be understood as a metaphor for a vastly larger creative process. Suffused with desire to pour love and goodness into a responsive universe, God 'speaks' Creation into existence by emanating surges of divine energy from within God's innermost Being. One could perhaps say that God 'ex-presses' Creation."

Rabbi Prager suggests that you "consider the process of speech in your own body. You want to say something, to offer your feelings or ideas. The wanting causes an energy to rise up within you. Your diaphragm rises, your stomach muscles tighten, and your breath waits in expectancy. Your body tenses lightly as it prepares to ex-press. Express what? Your *self*. To speak is to ex-press yourself. God 'speaks' and 'ex-presses' or 'presses out' God's *self*. From deep within the Infinite-Core-of-Being, wave after wave of energy pours forth."

So when you sit down to enjoy a meal, you have the opportunity to connect with this divine life force expressing itself through the nutritious food and through the remarkable ability you've been given to derive health and vitality from this food. You can strengthen your connection to this ongoing process of creation by taking a deep breath and saying the words "*Barookh Atah Adonai Eloheinu melekh ha-olam, sheh-hakol nih-hiyeh bid-varo*—Blessed are You, Eternal One, Energy Source of the universe, through Whose word or expression everything came to be." Then imagine that there is a mysterious desire or force inherent in the universe, a desire or force of a higher nature that wants this food to nourish you and help you share your gifts and your kindness with others. At a moment like this you might feel a part of the entire process of creation.

The Two-Way Directionality of a Prayer

There is one additional spiritual interpretation of the blessing at a meal that you might find interesting. This imagery may require a bit of faith, so if your rational mind says, "What's going on here—where's the proof?" you may need to gently reassure it that we're dealing in spiritual exploration here, not necessarily in hard-nosed scientific evidence.

This idea about food and prayer comes from Rabbi Isaac Luria, the sixteenth-century kabbalist mentioned in Chapter 1, who spoke eloquently about the holy sparks of light and energy that need to be raised up by our actions of *tikkun* or repair. Luria and his followers described how a two-way process happens in the cosmos when you or I say a heartfelt prayer.

On the one hand, saying a prayer of thanks to God for the food we are about to eat pulls in an energy flow of divine abundance, which in Hebrew is called *shefa*. This divine energy flow stirs up the sparks of holiness that are hidden in all things, including the food on your plate. It's as though the spiritual richness of the food gets unlocked when you remember to say a sincere blessing over it. And if you forget to say a prayer, it can block the flow or spiritual attunement that is a key to healthy living.

Rabbi Aryeh Kaplan in his book *Meditation and Kabbalah* describes how the prayer over food can draw down *shefa* and affect the food you are about to eat. He says, "My master teacher taught that when a person recites a blessing over food with *kavanah* (intention), he removes the restrictive spiritual husks or coverings from the food. In this manner, an individual purifies his body, making it spiritually transparent, prepared to receive holiness."

Luria and his followers, as described in the kabbalistic book *Pri Eytz Hadar (The Fruit of the Beautiful Tree)*, also believed that when you or I say a prayer over a meal and then eat with a holy intention, it can raise up the divine sparks contained in the cells of the food. Luria suggested that you can stir up the potency and loving-kindness of God or boost the ongoing creative flow of the universe when you sit down to a meal. Your words of prayer and the quality of your thoughts while eating can have an effect on higher levels of reality.

This mysterious process of stirring up and sending holy sparks of energy to higher levels of reality is explained in the book *The Essential Kabbalah* by Rabbi Daniel Matt. Paraphrasing from several Chasidic masters, Rabbi Matt suggests, "You can mend the cosmos by anything you do—even eating. Do not imagine that God wants you to eat for mere pleasure or to fill your belly. No, the purpose is mending. When you desire to eat or drink, or to fulfill other worldly desires, and you focus your awareness on the love of God, then you elevate your physical desire to spiritual desire. Thereby you bring forth holy sparks from the material world, from deep within the food and drink, and you serve God."

Now I can imagine one of my atheistic friends reading this and saying, "What are you talking about? Do you really believe that saying a prayer can make the food more nutritious or that this blessing can somehow raise up holy sparks to higher levels of the cosmos, where they will make an impact on divine energies?"

To this friend I would respond, "It doesn't matter whether you believe the spiritual imagery. If you stop on a hectic day and make sure that before you eat your meal you take a deep breath, say a blessing, and feel connected to the creative flow that brought this food to your fingertips, that alone will be enough to make the meal more healthy for your body. I can't prove whether there are divine sparks being aroused in the food or whether your prayer rises to higher levels of reality. But I can guarantee that your relaxed stomach muscles and the well-fed cells in your blood and body will thank you. I have seen dozens of individuals improve their digestive problems slightly or substantially by learning to unwind and connect with a sense of holiness at each meal. You might want to try it out for a while."

I can also imagine another friend of mine, a spiritual individual who believes in a loving Presence that expresses and creates in the world, who might ask, "How come no one ever taught me about these mystical interpretations for saying a blessing over food?"

To this friend I would say, "No one taught it to me either when I was little, so we would go on youth group retreats and say, 'Rub a dub dub, thanks for the grub, yea God,' like it was all a big joke. Or we would say the *motzi* prayer over and over like it was a boring singsong routine. No one thought in those days that kids could understand these rich ideas from the mystical side of Judaism. But today, when I ask my seven-year-old son, 'Do you ever feel God's love in the food we eat?' he smiles and says, 'Absolutely.' My son is convinced that there is a loving, creative force in the universe and that delicious food is one of the clues that we are enjoying God's presence. He and most kids are capable of understanding that there's an energy in the universe that has an effect on every aspect of our lives and that we human beings can affect this energy force somewhat by our acts of loving-kindness."

I offer both these choices as legitimate ways of experiencing the Jewish tradition of making each meal a holy moment. If you tend toward the skeptical, just know that your prayers are having an effect on your digestive process. And if you tend toward the believing side, consider that your blessings make an impact not only here on Earth but also on unseen levels of reality that you and I may never fully understand. Either way there are benefits from saying a prayer when you sit down to a meal. Now here's to your good health as you enjoy the fruits of creation.

In Your Own Words

Despite all the good spiritual and practical reasons for saying a blessing when you sit down for a meal, there is another aspect that gives people trouble. As described by one of my therapy clients, "It's the awkwardness of doing something religious or spiritual in public, like when you're at a restaurant, a shopping mall food court, or an outdoor meal in a city park. Especially the part of bowing your head or saying a prayer in Hebrew in a public setting. There are some people who don't have a problem being overtly Jewish in public, but I have to admit that I'm not one of them. I've always thought of my Jewishness as private and personal. It would be extremely awkward for me to be praying out loud in Hebrew where others might be looking and judging. I wish I didn't feel that way, but I do." Would it be awkward or embarrassing for you to be seen in public saying a prayer over food? Or even among close friends or family—is it uncomfortable to be seen closing your eyes and offering thanks to God?

Several of my friends, colleagues, and counseling clients have told me that they agreed in principle with saying a prayer before eating, but they still felt too uncomfortable to do it in front of other people. So I asked one of my clients, a somewhat shy and sensitive graduate student in her early twenties, "What would make it possible for you to say a prayer when you're around a judgmental family member or friend, or when you're in a restaurant or a public place?"

She thought it over and responded, "If I could say the blessing in my own words and if I then asked the other person to offer a blessing in his or her own words before eating, that would make me less self-conscious. Or if I'm alone at a meal, maybe I could just say the Hebrew words silently and then some of my own feelings of thanks silently to myself. That's really what I want to be doing—to be talking with God and not to be concerned about the strangers around me who might be wondering what's going on."

Here is the prayer she came up with, which she says silently if she's feeling self-conscious or out loud if she senses the people around her are open to praying before a meal. See if it sparks anything you might want to say to God when you sit down to eat a meal:

Thank you, dear God, for this food,

For the health and good energy it will give us,

And for all the men and women who helped grow and transport and serve this delicious offering.

Please help me to remember that this food is but one of a million different ways that Your creation nourishes and provides for us.

May I never forget what a miracle it is to be alive in a body that You've given me for doing good in the world.

May this food and this meal be used for blessing.

Amen.

If you set aside a few moments before each meal to say one of the traditional blessings or a spontaneous prayer in your own words, you will be giving your body a chance to unwind and fully benefit from the nourishment. I can't promise that this prayer will completely cure any heart or digestive problems you have, but I strongly believe it can improve your chances for a healthier outcome to whatever ails you. It can assist whatever else you are doing medically or with lifestyle changes to improve your body's health and vitality. Our bodies need to take in nourishment in a nonstressful atmosphere, and you might be surprised at how much your physical symptoms improve if you reduce the agitation you encounter at each meal.

In addition, if you begin to explore the mystery of praying and centering at each meal, you will be connecting with the incredible chain of ongoing creation that turns light, energy, and earth into foods that sustain us for doing good in the world. My hope is that each meal will satisfy not only your physical hunger but also your spiritual longing for connection and support. We human beings have numerous opportunities each day, each week, and each month to make this connection between good food and heartfelt spirituality. I hope these moments of prayer will be enjoyable for you and the people you care about with whom you break bread and share the journey of life.

CHAPTER FIVE

A Prayer to Help Heal the Body and the Soul of You or Someone You Love

Mi shebeirakh avoteinu	May the Source who blessed our ancestors
. . . v'yishlakh m'heirah	. . . send speedily
refu-ah sh'leimah min hashamayim . . .	a complete recovery from heaven . . .
refu-at ha-nefesh	a recovery of the spirit,
oo-refu-at ha-guf.	and a recovery of the body.

At a synagogue healing service held in Los Angeles, I watch as a wide variety of individuals chant a prayer for renewal of body and spirit for one of the congregants, who is seriously ill. A part of me is still skeptical and walled off from the group. We didn't have healing prayer services like this when I was growing up in Detroit. The strictly rational part of my brain finds it a little odd to be chanting an ancient Hebrew prayer and hoping it will help someone in modern times.

Yet another part of my mind is fascinated. This prayer for an ailing member of the congregation feels so passionate and sincere. Right now in this room there seems to be a deep sense of community. As the chanting continues the feeling is so strong that I'm beginning to wonder if the Shekhinah (the in-dwelling presence of the Eternal) might be moving through the words of the men and women around me to affect the body and soul of the person who has come for our support and prayers.

In the past few years healing prayer services of various types have begun to take place in all the branches of Judaism— Reform, Conservative, Orthodox, Reconstructionist, Renewal, and Chasidic. I look around and see several former atheists who five years ago wouldn't have believed that today they'd be standing in a circle of congregants asking God for healing for a dear friend. I also see several men and women who were raised in very strict Orthodox homes, where joining in a mixed prayer circle like this would be considered against the rules.

These healing prayers seem to touch all of the parti-cipants on a deeply human level. No matter what type of religious upbringing we had or didn't have, these prayers make all of us wonder, Is it possible? Can prayer really assist a man or woman to experience a dramatic improvement from a physical ailment?

After a few additional minutes of chanting the traditional "Mi shebeirakh" prayer (which means "To the One who brings blessing"), I begin to sense something has shifted. I can't put words on it, but something feels very different when the prayer is over than it did when the prayer began. It might be a mystical sense of how prayer sometimes opens up avenues of healing and connection. Seeing the face of the person being prayed for (whose disease did go into remission a few weeks after the heartfelt prayers said for her benefit) makes me more curious than ever about the mysterious power of sacred words and rituals.

Walking the Fine Line Between
False Hope and Realistic Wonder

This chapter is difficult to write. On the one hand, I don't want to be a false optimist who insists that prayer always heals whatever ails us. I believe this type of guarantee is dishonest and might cause harm to people who would feel let down after praying sincerely and finding that nothing has changed in their physical condition. As you probably have experienced in your own life, sometimes even the most passionate and profound words of prayer cannot change a situation that is beyond reversal. Since illness and physical death are part of the overall design of the universe, our task as humans is to search for meaning and purpose in even the most difficult moments.

On the other hand, I don't want to underestimate the healing potential of our prayers. When we pray for energies of recovery and renewal to emerge from within the soul of someone (including yourself) who is ailing, it's a leap of faith that sometimes leads to mysterious and wonderful breakthroughs. There are no guarantees, but I have seen some amazing results that coincided with prayers directly intended to assist in the healing of someone who deeply desires a renewal of body and spirit.

So my goal for this chapter is to present a few perspectives on healing that you and your loved ones can consider. I don't have an easy answer as to exactly how prayer works on the physical body, but I can provide some insights that might stir your own thoughts. These insights come from experts in spirituality and psychology, as well as from the current research findings of psychoneuroimmunology (the science of how the mind and body interact in health and illness). You will be surprised at the similarity between what the scientific folks and the spiritual folks are saying about the mystery of healing. By the end of the chapter, you will have gained greater awareness of what might be happening when we pray for healing and how to tune in to this mystical process on a deeper level.

Rediscovering a Most Unusual Prayer

It's strange how you can hear a prayer over and over and it doesn't move you. But then one day you hear it during an unguarded moment, and the prayer grabs you. It's as though you are open to the deeper energies of this prayer for the first time.

Like many people, I had heard the "Mi shebeirakh" prayer recited, mumbled, and raced through hundreds of times. Here's a shortened English version: "May the One who blessed our ancestors, Abraham, Isaac and Jacob, Sarah, Rebecca, Rachel and Leah, bless and heal ————. May the Holy One in mercy strengthen him (her) and heal him (her) soon, with a complete *Refu-ah sh'leimah,* a restoring of body and soul, together with others who suffer illness. And let us say: Amen."

If you've ever been to a traditional Saturday morning Torah service or a High Holiday service where people come forward to say a blessing in front of the open Torah scroll, you probably have heard someone say these words quickly and without much emotion: *"Mi shebeirakh avohteinu Avra-*

ham, Yitzhak, v'Ya-akov . . .—May the One who blessed our ancestors Abraham, Isaac, and Jacob. . . ." In most congregations this fast recitation usually is given as a reward to someone who's contributed a lot of money to the synagogue or someone who is very active in the community.

Or if the congregation has a tradition of stopping during the Torah service to say a prayer for those who are ill, you may have seen the rabbi or a prayer leader saying very quickly, *"Mi shebeirakh avohteinu Avraham, Yitzhak, v'Ya-akov. . . ."* If you've never studied this prayer in depth, you may have wondered, What is this ancient prayer for healing all about, and why does it start with our ancestors Abraham, Isaac, Jacob, Moses, Aaron, David, and Solomon (and in many congregations Sarah, Rebecca, Rachel, Leah, and others)?

According to Macy Nulman, author of *The Encyclopedia of Jewish Prayer,* this tradition of a major contributor or honored member of the community standing at the open Torah scroll and calling for a blessing upon the community and upon loved ones who are ill by reciting the "Mi shebeirakh" prayer goes as far back as Babylonian Jewry in the sixth century. It essentially asks the divine source of healing and blessing to give special consideration to a community or an individual in need because of the accumulated merit of the person requesting this help and because of the inherent merit of the community reading and studying from the Torah together. The tradition says that the good deeds and spiritual study we perform (and that were performed by our ancestors) can help bring assistance to those who are in need of blessing.

But, to be honest, sitting in the congregation and hearing these words spoken in a mumbled rush never gave me a personal sense that deep healing or spiritual transformation was occurring. As a result I'd never experienced the "Mi shebeirakh" prayer as a mystical avenue for healing until a number of years ago when my wife, Linda, and I happened to be at a concert where the singer-songwriter Debbie Friedman sang her soulful version of this traditional blessing and many in the audience (including Linda and I) were moved to tears. If you've never heard her rendition of the "Mi shebeirakh" prayer, I recommend buying one of the CDs or tapes that have it (see Appendix B).

Now when I hear the words, *"Mi shebeirakh avoteinu—* May the Source who blessed our ancestors . . . bless this person with a renewal of body and spirit," I sometimes feel as though I am traveling to an unseen level of consciousness where holy energies, fate, vulnerability, and the journey of our souls are being worked out in ways that are beyond human comprehension. This prayer seems to be about far more than a Band-Aid or a pill. It seems to be about a type of healing that mystics have talked about for centuries but that science is only beginning to study and understand.

So for the past several years I have begun saying the "Mi shebeirakh" prayer whenever I have felt concerned about an ailing loved one, friend, or counseling client, as well as for times when I was ill myself. It has sometimes felt a little awkward at first to be calling out to an invisible Source for help regarding a physical or emotional ailment. But many times when I've taken a deep breath and prayed with serious intention for the healing or recovery of someone I care about, I have felt a mysterious sense of oneness with a loving Presence that is beyond words.

In Appendix A I list some of the recent research findings about prayer and healing. I want to reemphasize that there is no guarantee this prayer will reverse a physical or mental illness, which often has a momentum of its own. But I have come to believe that something important and beneficial might be happening when individuals or a spiritual gathering reach deep into their hearts to recite these ancient words for stirring up sparks of renewal and strength.

The Spiritual Components of Healing

Each time I've said the "Mi shebeirakh" prayer, either alone or in a gathering, has made me curious about what this traditional prayer really means and why it has served for so many centuries as one of the key prayers for healing in the Jewish tradition. What exactly is meant by "a recovery of spirit and body"? I wanted to know if our tradition felt it was permissible to call out passionately for healing assistance or whether this might be considered too selfish or too demanding. I also wanted to know what the phrase *refu-ah sh'leimah* (usually translated as "complete healing") means in practical terms and what the idea of "God's mercy" refers to from a Jewish perspective.

So I began to study various teachings about this ancient blessing. I found that if you seriously explore these questions about the "Mi Shebeirakh" prayer, you will gain a much deeper insight into the process of healing. Here are a few ideas for you and your loved ones to consider.

What Does Refu-ah Sh'leimah Mean on Several Levels?

Most Hebrew-English dictionaries define *refu-ah* as "healing" or "health," while *sh'leimah* (like *shalom*) means "wholeness or completeness." As a result the phrase *refu-ah sh'leimah* often gets translated as "complete healing."

At first glance this "complete healing" would seem to mean we are praying for an external God to step in and remove all the symptoms of illness. It sounds like a request for God to take over and make it possible for us to wake up the next day with the entire bad episode gone. This notion of "complete healing" is almost a childlike wish for a magical divine intervention.

This one-sidedness is *not* the way most Jewish texts on healing describe God's involvement in *refu-ah sh'leimah*. For example, if you read any of the books on Jewish perspectives regarding illness and healing that are listed in Appendix B, you will find that Jewish tradition has consistently looked at the divine-human partnership as a *combined* effort for healing. Judaism has historically viewed God as the primary healing force, which mysteriously transmits energies of repair and renewal through a variety of cocreators: gifted doctors and nurses, remarkable remedies and technologies, highly motivated patients, and deeply concerned loved ones—friends, relatives, and community members whose *bikkur kholim* (visits to an ill person) are essential to helping heal. In most Jewish writings on the subject, it's not a magical one-sided external intervention but a powerful partnership that once again shows how an invisible Divine Presence expresses love and healing through human acts of loving-kindness.

This concept of *refu-ah sh'leimah* is similar to what psychological research and medical studies are now identifying as the keys to health and well-being. Whereas a few decades ago many people thought you could be passive and let the doctors, with their extensive training and high-tech devices, do the healing, now we know from numerous studies that several additional factors make a successful recovery far more likely. One study after another has shown that the patient's attitude, prayer, sense of humor, sense of community and family support, and willingness to do everything possible to commit to a healthy lifestyle dramatically improve the chances of recovery or remission from cancer, heart disease, strokes, alcoholism, drug addiction, AIDS, diabetes, multiple sclerosis, and many other acute and chronic conditions.

In addition, the phrase *refu-ah sh'leimah* often *does not* mean that the illness has been magically removed from the person. In the childlike, passive image of "complete healing" described earlier, the person would be praying for God to yank the cancer or the heart disease from the body once and for all. But if you study medicine, especially holistic medicine or the Eastern and Oriental traditions of healing, you will find that once-and-for-all removal of symptoms is not usually how our bodies work.

According to holistic and Oriental medicine, a return to wholeness or a renewal of health often *includes* the fact that the underlying risk factors, genetic markers, and propensities for illness might still be in our bodies but are now in remission and we can live fully as long as we remain conscious of how to stay balanced and healthy one day at a time.

This commonsense approach corresponds to the essential Jewish view of how a daily renewal of body and spirit occurs, as described by the Chasidic rabbi Abraham Twersky in his book *Living Each Day*. Twersky writes that when we pray for healing, we shouldn't expect God to take away all the underlying vulnerabilities that make us human but rather to give us guidance and strength to help us attune or align ourselves each day with the best spiritual and medical wisdom for how to stay on track toward our healthiest potential. Every human being is at risk for one or several illnesses—that fact is a part of our genes, our environment, and our underlying susceptibilities.

That's why Jewish teachings suggest that when we pray we're not denying or ignoring these vulnerabilities but asking for higher wisdom on how to find the right frame of mind, the right doctors and nurses, the right treatment plans, the right remedies, the right prevention and maintenance steps, and the right emotional and physical support for our day-to-day recoveries. Twersky and many other Jewish teachers would say that prayer is *not* about hiding from our human susceptibilities but rather for taking action to respond most effectively to them. To pray for healing doesn't mean to ask for a different body or a different soul than the one you were born with; instead it opens you up to a renewed daily boost of wisdom and support from divine and human sources.

So maybe "complete healing" is not the only way to translate the words *refu-ah sh'leimah*. At the University of Judaism's

Ostrow Library in Los Angeles, I went looking for a definitive translation of *refu-ah sh'leimah* and found a microfiche copy of a well-documented 1985 Ph.D. dissertation by an expert on Near Eastern languages from New York University. This dissertation studied the linguistic roots of the word *refu-ah* to find a translation that most closely reflected how it was used in the Hebrew Bible and in the Hebrew and Aramaic dialects of the ancient Near East.

The author demonstrated that *refu-ah* should not be translated as just "to heal," as though it meant the final removal of all symptoms. Rather the ancient word *refu-ah* describes an ongoing process by which something or someone is gradually "restored to wholeness," "is made whole from a broken condition," "is sewn or patched together," or "is joined or brought together." This notion of renewal allows an ailing person to feel fully alive and connected to God even while he or she is facing a chronic condition or a recurring illness.

For a psychologist like myself, who frequently counsels ailing people and those whose illnesses are in remission, this version of *refu-ah sh'leimah* as helping someone to gradually become whole again after feeling broken makes a lot of sense. When I've counseled people with cancer, heart problems, strokes, AIDS, lupus, fibromyalgia, skin disorders, diabetes, multiple sclerosis, arthritis, and other ailments, it has felt somewhat fanciful and dishonest to have them pray for "a complete healing," because both the patient and I were fully aware that there is always a risk of flare-ups.

What seems more useful, accurate, and empowering is to pray for "a return to wholeness" or "a recovery from feeling broken," both of which say to the ailing person, "It's better to live each day with a continued awareness of how fragile our health is and how important it is to stay balanced and on track than to close your eyes and hope that some outside intervention will make you into a completely different person. Having an illness (that either is active or dormant at the moment) doesn't make you deficient or broken. You pray for and strive toward a return to wholeness, a renewal of body and spirit, even in the midst of your daily ups and downs."

As one of my counseling clients, who has a severe immune system disorder, told me recently, "When I used to pray to God to magically remove all my symptoms, I'd invariably wind up feeling let down and alienated from God each time the symptoms reappeared. But now, when I pray for God's guidance and support on how to stay balanced and renewed each day so I don't retrigger my disorder, I feel nurtured and assisted by God's loving presence. Every single day this 'Mi shebeirakh' prayer helps me experience a much-needed renewal of body and spirit, even though my immune system is still quite fragile and in need of careful maintenance."

Another of my counseling clients is a woman in her forties who used the "Mi shebeirakh' prayer to ask for wholeness, strength, and healing energies for her young daughter, who has severe developmental disabilities. This client told me, "When I used to pray for a 'complete healing' for my daughter's disabilities, I came away each time feeling disappointed that the disabilities were still there. That's because I used to think of 'complete healing' as a magic wand to make my daughter into a completely different person."

She continues, "But now when I use the 'Mi shebeirakh' blessing to pray for strength, wholeness, and healing of body and spirit for my daughter and for myself, I see there are signs the prayer is working. I notice my daughter's spirit and her energies are stronger the more I pray for her. I also notice my own resilience and effectiveness as a caregiver are stronger when I focus on wholeness and on seeing her soul and my soul moving on a long path toward healing. My prayers are no longer an attempt to deny what clearly is or to insist that there's only one way for healing of body and spirit to occur. Rather, my prayers are now a source of constant strength for making small steps of progress each and every day."

Therefore, as you think about your own ailments or those of a loved one, consider asking the Divine Presence for a daily boost of healing energy and strength. This *refu-ah sh'leimah* (return to wholeness) allows you to feel profoundly alive and on track toward continued healing of body and spirit *even if* there are ups and downs with your symptoms. Your soul and your spiritual strength can remain intact even if your body has good days and hard days. This is one of the greatest benefits of prayer—that even on the toughest days you can solidify your connection to the healing energies around you and within you. When you pray with sincerity for a return to wholeness, you can feel at one with the Divine Presence that lives within your soul. Instead of feeling alienated or distant from the supportive energies of the Eternal One, you can feel close to the source of strength.

Could Illness Be an Indication That God Is Punishing the Ill Person?

I hesitate even to ask this question, but since it arises for so many men and women, it's important to address this very human concern. We live in a world where people are continually speculating on "what God intends." It might be a relative or friend who responds to your illness or someone else's ailments by saying, "Well, maybe God is trying to send you a message." Or it might be a spiritual healer or guru who insists, "The reason you have that illness is God's trying to wake you up." Or a part of your own mind might contain the fear "Maybe this is God's way of punishing me for when I did ———."

I certainly cannot speculate on what God intends for any of us or why horrible illnesses happen to good people. In fact, in Jewish tradition many scholars and rabbis suggest that it's pointless to ask why? or why me? of an illness. These teachers recommend that it's far more useful to ask what now? or what can be done? to respond with dignity and compassion to the painful things that happen to all of us at some time in our lives. The relevant question is not "Why is this illness flaring up—what did I do wrong?" but rather "What can be done to turn this illness into an opportunity for learning, growth, loving-kindness, and a renewal of body and spirit?"

However, what if you were raised in a family, a community, or a synagogue where illness was viewed as "God's judgment"? To help you or your loved one overcome this widespread view of illness or suffering, I would like to offer a fascinating interpretation presented in the journal *Sh'ma,* which has scholars and readers from all parts of Judaism, including Orthodox, Conservative, Reform, Reconstructionist, Renewal, and others. This explanation of God's role in our illnesses was written in 1994 by Rabbi Nancy Flam, a director of the National Center for Jewish Healing, with offices in San Francisco and New York. Rabbi Flam specializes in assisting men and women from all branches of Judaism to respond to illness from a Jewish spiritual perspective. Since many people tend to ask during an illness, Was this somehow a punishment or a judgment from God for something I did wrong? Rabbi Flam offers a tradition-based teaching called "Reflections Toward a Theology of Illness and Healing."

According to the ancient rabbis, God's powerful influence in our lives was characterized by the Hebrew word *din,* which usually gets translated "judgment" or "justice." You might recognize the word *din* from the common phrase *Beit Din,* which often refers to a panel of three rabbis who judge or rule on Jewish divorces, conversions, or on matters of potential disagreement.

But there's another equally valid way of looking at God's role as the ruling force in the physical universe. As Rabbi Flam explains, "When an illness or death happens, I think the element of *din* is here. By this I do *not* mean 'judgment' or 'justice' in the way the rabbis usually mean it. I mean a morally neutral *din: din* as the imposition of limits, the correct determination of things, the *din* that Moses Cordovera (a sixteenth-century Kabbalist leader in Safed in Galilee) talks about as inherent in all things in so far as *all things need to remain what they are, to stay within their boundaries.*" (For example, that we humans need to live within our limits as mortal beings, not because God is "judging" or "punishing" us but simply because those are the boundaries of who we are.)

Rabbi Flam explains, "*Midat ha-din* (the divine attribute of *din* or limit-setting), then, carries within it the necessity of limits and finitude. Disease and death are expressions of *midat ha-din*. Physical bodies are limited; they are created with a finite capacity for life and health. They are vulnerable to disease, injury, and decay. We are created and, without exception, pass away. This is part of God's holy design."

She continues,

> Whereas illness expresses *midat ha-din* (the divine attribute of *din* or limit-setting), healing expresses *midat ha-rakhamim* (the divine attribute of mercy). *Rakhamim* is classically envisioned as the force which mitigates the severity of the *din;* in cases where *midat ha-din* (divine limit-setting) would exact strict limits, *midat ha-rakhamim* (divine mercy or nurturance) comes to soften the decree. *Rakhamim* makes it possible for us to live within the reality of *din.* The two principles work together in the formation and daily re-creation of the world.
>
> To my mind, this is indeed how the world works. Our human acts of mercy, compassion, and empathy make it possible for us to endure, to suffer the sometimes excruciatingly painful limits and losses of creation. We may not be able to make disease disappear, but we can profoundly

affect how we cope with illness, thereby 'softening the decree,' if you will.

Our classic Jewish sources speak of the power of *rakhamim* (acts of mercy) to affect the realm of *din* (limits). As if our very human love, compassion, and empathy, as well as our research, science, and treatment could move nature to overcome previously known limits. As if our love, our presence, our bestowal of dignity could heal both spiritually and physically.

Rabbi Flam concludes, "I do not suggest that *din* (limits) ought to be or even could be eliminated entirely. The same *midrash* (rabbinic discussion) which says that the world cannot be ruled by pure *din* (limits) also says that it would not stand if guided only by *rakhamim* (mercy). But our desire, our vision, is to move the world toward holding a greater share of *rakhamim* than of *din*. Even God is imagined to exclaim in Berkahot 7a [a Talmudic book of ancient rabbinic insights], 'O that I might forever let my mercy prevail over my justice.'"

In other words, Rabbi Flam and many other scholars look at illness not as a punishment but as a reflection of the inherent limit setting that makes us human. So when you pray to God about your illness or the illness of someone you love, you need to choose which sense of God you are addressing. Is it the God who judges and punishes? Or is it the two-sided energy of *din* (limit setting) and *rakhamim* (mercy) that you want to connect with for support?

If your prayer is directed toward the loving Presence that also sets limits, you might ask, "Please God, extend this limit. In your great compassion, give this body and this spirit a renewed flow of your healing energy." In this way God is not your punitive enemy during an illness but rather your connection to the pulsing life force that exists both within us and around us. Instead of being at war with God, you can breathe in the deep compassion of the Eternal One, who creates life and sometimes extends the limits or softens them with human and divine acts of mercy.

Is It Permissible to Ask the Infinite Source for One Individual to Be Helped?

This final question about the "Mi shebeirakh" prayer has been raised by many of my counseling clients, who often ask, "How does it work when the Divine Presence has so many people in need all over the world? Isn't it self-centered to be asking God's intervention for just one individual?"

Judaism offers several useful explanations of how to view the process of healing and the abundance of energy you can draw upon when you pray for help. One of my favorites is the double-sided idea of how Jewish teachings view the individual human being. On the one hand, we human beings are to view ourselves and others with humility—that we are like tiny drops of water in a huge ocean. On the other hand, there is an ancient Jewish teaching which says that the world was created for the sake of a single individual and that if you save one life you save an entire world (because that one life eventually will affect an entire universe of people and situations).

The passage from the ancient rabbis says: "Therefore only a single human being was created in the world to teach that if any person has caused a single soul to perish, the Bible regards him as if he has caused an entire world to perish; and if any human being saves a single soul, the Bible regards him as if he had saved an entire world."

So calling out to God to ask for a renewal of body and spirit for one individual is extremely permissible and important. After all, each of us might be just a drop in a huge ocean, but we are also, each of us, created in the image of the Divine, so to save a life is to cherish and renew a spark of the Eternal One.

A second teaching on whether it's permissible to call out passionately to God for assisting one ailing person comes from the Sabbath liturgy. During the weekdays we are instructed to engage in *tikkun olam,* to repair the brokenness of ourselves and the world. But on Sabbath we are to refrain from all work, including any attempts to change God's creation—Sabbath is a day for resting and connecting without any meddling, a day set aside for rehearsing what life will be like when everyone has enough and nothing more needs to be fixed. Therefore, tradition says that on Sabbath you can offer prayers of thanks and prayers that bless, but you're not to offer petitions or requests to make things different from how they are.

The major exception on Sabbath is if you want to call out a prayer for healing. In synagogues around the world throughout history it has been permissible to ask God to save a life or to restore to wholeness the body and spirit of anyone who has been ailing. There is even a line in the traditional version of the prayer in which we say on the Sabbath to God: "Please send this person a recovery of the body and a recovery of the spirit though the Sabbath prohibits us from crying out, may a recovery come speedily, swiftly, and soon." Saving a life takes precedence over halting all world-altering activity on the Sabbath. So once again the tradition seems to be saying it is extremely permissible to ask the Divine Presence to help those who are in need of healing.

Nonetheless, I have often heard from therapy clients, friends, and colleagues that they feel "a little embarrassed" to be asking God for assistance for one person's aches and pains. Maybe it's good to feel a bit of shyness—in this world of narcissists and "me-me-me" pushiness, a moment of humility is like a breath of fresh air. If you're feeling a little uncomfortable asking the Creator of the universe (or the Divine Presence who dwells within) for assistance with one person's messy medical situation, just accept that we are all like drops of water in a huge ocean. But at the same time remember the other side of the human identity—we are sparks of the Divine and to save a single life is to save an entire world.

Please don't hold back when your heart wants assistance for the illness you or someone you care about is suffering. Jewish tradition gives you complete permission to call out for the source of healing to emerge from deep within our souls so that we might once again be restored to wholeness. Don't hesitate to say the "Mi shebeirakh" prayer with strong intention.

Connecting Charity with Prayers for Healing

There is an additional tradition that has a fascinating set of meanings, which you will also want to consider while praying for the recovery or health of yourself or someone you love. Judaism has a well-established tradition of giving charity soon after saying the "Mi shebeirakh" prayer. I have heard many interpretations of why the practice of giving a small or large donation to a nonprofit group or needy individual is attached to this prayer for healing. Here are two versions for you to consider.

One is that the act of giving to a charity in honor of an ailing person creates merit for that individual and thus draws attention to summon God's energies for assisting this person's recovery and care. The charity and its recipients benefit from your desire to honor and assist someone you care about; in addition, your loved one benefits because you are making a declaration to God that this person's recovery is so important you are willing to take action and improve one aspect of the world on this person's behalf.

Another of the interpretations I like best says that the reason to be generous is that all our souls are connected in the great womb of life. The Hebrew word *rekhem* for womb has the same root word as *rakhamim* (divine mercy or nurturance), which on a spiritual level means that when you or I need some support we should remember that being a soul in the world is like living within the nurturing, developing womb of the Eternal Life Force. That may sound strange to your rational mind, but if you could ask a fish what it's like to live in water the fish would say, "What are you talking about?" So it is with human beings—we can't really see with our eyes the divine support and nurturance that surround us and flow within us. Most people grow up thinking of God as a judge or a ruler, but in fact many of the teachings and prayers in Judaism refer to God's *rakhmones,* or to God as Ha-rakhamon, which translate "womb," "protector," "nurturing life force," "compassionate One" or "merciful One."

According to the mystical tradition in Judaism, when you give to charity to help another individual or group in the connected womb of life, your act stirs up an additional healing flow of energy for other individuals as well. The energy flow of *rakhamim* stirred up by your heartfelt act will therefore increase the healing energies within the person for whom you are praying.

The next time you give a small or large donation of time or money to a charity that creates more justice in the world, imagine yourself stirring up an invisible channel of healing energy. This channel of healing energy opens not only your own heart but also the flow of mercy and repair throughout the universe. It's like singing a soulful melody in an echo chamber—you just might be opening up your own heart as well as sending a vibration of melodic sound that bounces back continually and affects all those within the same acoustic field.

Saying the Prayer with Commitment and Understanding

Now that we've looked at the "Mi shebeirakh" prayer from the psychological, medical, and spiritual perspectives, here are the actual words you can say—either alone, in a congregation at services, or in a prayer group focused on healing. Since the prayer is somewhat long, you may need to familiarize yourself with the words a few times before you are ready to say it with all your heart and soul.

When saying the prayer for a woman who needs healing

Mi shebeirakh avoteinu	May the One who blessed our forefathers,
Avraham, Yitzhak, v'Ya-akov,	Abraham, Isaac, and Jacob,
Moshe, Aharon, Daveed, oo-Shlomo	Moses, Aaron, David, and Solomon,
v'imoteinu Sara, Rivkah, Rakhel, v'Leah	and our foremothers Sarah, Rebecca, Rachel, and Leah,
hoo y'varekh vi-rah-peh et ha-khola	may the One bless and heal this person
(add the person's Hebrew name if you can)	(or the person's English name)
bat	daughter of
(the person's mother's Hebrew name)	(or the person's mother's English name)

ba-avoor sheh	because
(your Hebrew name if you know it)	(or your English name)
yitain litz'dakah ba-avoorah.	will contribute to charity on her behalf.
Bis'khar zeh,	In response to this,
Ha-kadosh Barookh Hoo yimalei	may the Holy One, Blessed are You,
rakhamim ahleiha l'ha-khalimah	compassionately help her recover,
ool'rapotah, ool'ha-khazeekah	to heal her, to strengthen her,
ool'ha-khah-yotah.	and to revive her.
V'yish-lakh lah m'heirah	And may God send her speedily
refu-ah sh'leimah min hashamayim,	a return to wholeness from heaven
l'khal eivah-reh-ha, ool'khal gihdeha	for all her organs and blood vessels,
b'tokh sh'ahr kholei yisra-el,	among the other ailing people of Israel
refu-at ha-nefesh, oo-refu-at ha-guf,	a renewal of spirit and of body,
hash'tah ba'agalah oovizmahn kareev.	(on the Sabbath and Festivals you add: Though the Sabbath/ Festival prohibits us from cry- ing out, may a recovery come speedily) swiftly and soon.
V'nohmar, Amen.	Now let us respond, Amen.

When saying the prayer for a man who needs healing

Mi shebeirakh avoteinu Avraham, Yitzhak,	May the One who blessed our forefathers Abraham, Isaac,
v'Ya-akov, Moshe, Aharon, Daveed, oo-Shlomo	and Jacob, Moses, Aaron, David, and Solomon,
v'imoteinu Sara, Rivkah, Rakhel, v'Leah,	and our foremothers Sarah, Rebecca, Rachel, and Leah,
hoo y'varekh vi-rah-peh et ha-kholeh	may the One bless and heal this person
(add the person's Hebrew name if you know it)	(or the person's English name)
ben	son of
(the person's mother's Hebrew name)	(or the person's mother's English name)
ba-avoor sheh	because
(your Hebrew name if you know it)	(or your English name)
yitain litz'dakah bah-avooroh.	will contribute to charity on his behalf.
Bis'khar zeh,	In response to this,
Ha-kadosh Barookh Hoo yimalei	May the Holy One, Blessed are You,
Rakhamim alahv, l'ha-khaleemo	compassionately help him recover,
ool'rahpotoh ool'ha-khazeeko	to heal him, to strengthen him,

ool'ha-kha-yotoh.	and to revive him.
V'yish-lakh lo m'heirah	And may God send him speedily
refu-ah sh'leimah min hashamayim,	a return to wholeness from heaven
lir'makh eivarav,	for his 248 organs
oosh'sah gidahv	and 365 blood vessels,
b'tokh sh'ahr kholei yisra-el,	among the other ailing people in Israel
refu-aht ha-nefesh, oo-refu-aht ha-guf,	a renewal of spirit and of body,
hash'tah ba'agalah oovizmahn kareev.	(on the Sabbath and Festivals you add: Though the Sabbath/ Festival prohibits us from crying out, may a recovery come speedily) swiftly and soon.
V'nohmar, Amen.	Now let us respond, Amen.

A Few Alternatives to Consider

In addition to the "Mi shebeirakh" prayer, there are several other spiritual ways to stir up energies of healing and repair for someone who is ailing. For instance, many prayer groups chant or recite several times the healing request made in the Book of Numbers (12:13) by Moses for his sister Miriam, *"Eil nah refah nah lah*—Please God, I pray, heal her now." This direct request for God to intervene has been an inspiring chant for many Jews throughout the centuries.

Rabbi Aryeh Hirschfield of Portland, Oregon, has written a beautiful melody and an inspiring variation on this prayer, which can be sung or recited alone or in a group. (While the prayer grammatically asks for the healing for a woman—Miriam—it can be said or sung *Eil nah refah nah lah* for both men and women.) When repeated several times it seems to have a way of deepening the prayerful energies:

From deep within the home of my soul,

Now let the healing, let the healing begin.

Ah nah, Eil nah, refah nah lah. Ah nah, Eil nah, refah nah lah.

Ah nah, Eil nah, refah nah lah. Ah nah, Eil nah, refah nah lah.

Heal our bodies, open our hearts, awaken our minds, Shekhinah.

Heal our bodies, open our hearts, awaken our minds, Eh-hih-yeh.

(I've found that when a group sings or chants these words over and over again, the sense of healing and connection can be quite strong.)

There is also a traditional prayer for healing in the daily liturgy. It comes near the end of the prayer service as one of the Eighteen Blessings (the Shemonei Esrei), often referred to as the Amidah (Standing Prayer). Once again, you may need to practice the words a few times until they become familiar so that you can say the prayer with deep intention for healing.

The traditional version says:

Refah-einu Adonai v'nei-rafeh,

hohshee-einu v'nivahshei-ah, kee t'hilahteinu atah,

v'ha-alei refu-ah sh'leimah l'khal mahcoteinu,

kee Eil melekh rofei neh-ehmahn v'rakhamahn atah. Barookh atah Adonai, rofei kholei ahmoh yisra-el.

Heal us, Eternal One, then we will be healed; save us—then we will be saved, for You are our prayer. Bring complete recovery for all our ailments, for You are God, ruling force, the faithful and compassionate Healer. Blessed are You, Eternal One, Who repairs the ailing of Your people Israel.

Finally, there is a teaching from the Chasidic Rabbi Nachman of Bratslav, who was the great-grandson of the founder of the Chasidic movement, the Baal Shem Tov, and whose writings and lectures have inspired millions of Jews for the past two hundred years. Rabbi Nachman identified ten psalms as having remarkable powers for helping a person heal the body and the spirit. These psalms, which are spelled out and discussed in an excellent recent book by Rabbi Simkha Weintraub of the National Center for Jewish Healing (see Appendix B), are 16, 32, 41, 42, 59, 77, 90, 105, 137, and 150. I've found that when an ailing person or a concerned caregiver uses these ancient poems of sadness, joy, longing, and renewal to call out to God for help, they can be extremely beneficial.

When you or someone else is ailing, so many things can spin your mind into fear, anxiety, and agitation. That's why it's important to have available several ways to refocus your mind and rechannel your efforts toward wholeness and recovery. One of the things I like about the use of psalms during a quest for healing is that these ancient poems call out both the pain and the hopefulness we feel at times of illness. If you've never utilized psalms to put words on your desire for a connection with God or your hope for assistance from God, these ten recommended psalms are a valuable way to begin.

In Your Own Words

Each human being has a slightly different way of talking with God. Especially when you or someone you love is ailing, conversations with the Infinite One are extremely personal and intense. So I hesitate to tell you what specific words to use. They must come from deep inside your heart.

But I will pass along a few examples from counseling clients who told me the precise ways they connected with the divine flow of healing energies that are around us and within us. Perhaps their passionately felt words will stimulate your own ideas about what you want to say to the One who creates us with both the capacity for illness and the capacity for healing and renewal. Here are the words recommended by men and women whom I have counseled and whom I respect enormously:

Barry is a man in his sixties who prays several times each day for the continued recovery of his wife, Karen, who was diagnosed with a terminal illness but is still alive six years after her doctors predicted she would probably die. Barry explains, "I grew up without much connection to God or religion. But in the past few years I've begun to take courses and visit different congregations. Lately Karen and I have begun to feel at home in one particular congregation where the people are sincere and the rabbi has a beautiful way of making the rituals meaningful and profound."

With the rabbi's help Barry developed a daily prayer ritual for asking God's assistance for Karen's recovery and for helping Barry's efforts to stay positive and energetic as her primary caregiver. According to Barry, "Each morning I make sure to sit in a quiet place in our living room for a few minutes and feel the pulsing energy of the universe. Slowly and carefully I then begin to repeat the ancient chant, *'Eil nah, refah nah lah*—Please God heal her now.'

At first I notice my mind is distracted, and sometimes I start worrying about Karen with all sorts of awful scenarios running through my head. But after a few minutes of chanting the prayer while breathing in and out, I begin to relax a bit. That's usually when I start to imagine God's light and healing warmth repairing the cells in my wife's body. I've always had a strong visual imagination, and at times I can actually see rays of light doing their work on Karen's cells. I have no idea if this is really happening on a physical level, but in my mind's eye the sense of God's light helping her continued recovery is quite vivid."

Barry adds, "Occasionally Karen and I pray together. I'm sorry we didn't start doing this a long time ago because it's quite intimate and loving to be sitting quietly in the living room and taking turns saying what's on our minds to God. At times Karen simply talks with God about what's been frustrating or difficult recently because of her illness. At other times we take turns talking with God about how much we both appreciate life and want God's help to make each day precious and meaningful. Sometimes I look over at my wife talking with God and my eyes fill with tears. It's so amazing to be sharing these intense moments with her. Her illness and recovery have taken our marriage to a deeper level of commitment than we've ever thought possible."

Debra is a forty-two-year-old single woman whose mother and sister both died of a rare genetic illness. Debra has had a few of the early symptoms of this ailment, but she has for the most part been able to continue functioning as a university professor.

During one of our counseling sessions, Debra told me that she has begun to pray at least several times a week, using these or similar words: "Please, God, help me and guide me today on how to expand the healing life force in my body. If I am drawn to any thoughts, foods, stresses, or habits that can trigger health problems, please give me the wisdom and the self-discipline to steer clear of these hazards. I love life, and I want to continue to be of service every day of my life. Please, God, may I be drawn to healing energies and to people and situations that nourish the gifts you've given me. Amen."

Jeremy has been visiting at least once a week his father, David, who was diagnosed with Alzheimer's disease eight years ago and has been declining ever since. David says, "My dad's former personality is pretty much gone now, and he has trouble knowing who's visiting him. But when I look into his eyes or I hold his hand, I can still feel the strong pulse within him, and I can sense his soul is still very much alive inside his withering body.

"So I recite the 'Mi shebeirakh' prayer with the intention of asking God to give my father a renewal of body and a renewal of spirit each day. Sometimes I do sense his body seems more relaxed and his soul seems to be more at peace when I stroke his head and say the prayer softly in front of him. In fact, one time when I was saying the words 'Please give my father a renewal of body and a renewal of spirit,' I saw his face soften and gently smile. It felt like a holy moment, to be able to get so close to my father and to sense that he was being comforted on a mysterious and deep level."

Jeremy concludes, "Near the end of the 'Mi shebeirakh' prayer, I like to add a few lines asking God to give strength and compassion to the men and women who are caring for my father at this nursing facility where he's been the past few years. There are a few truly outstanding individuals, who usually find a way to make my father more comfortable and less alone each day. These caregivers are God's agents in the world, and when I say the 'Mi shebeirakh' prayer, I like to add, 'Please bless the souls, the families, and the lives of these men and women who are so willing to be your vehicles for loving-kindness in my father's portion of the world. Please help all of these generous and compassionate individuals to know just how valuable they are as they bring

Your caring and Your strength to each of these patients who depend on them so much. Amen.'"

Gina is an experienced nurse who works in a midsized hospital that has recently been taken over by a large company from another state. According to Gina, "There is so much budget cutting and office politics going on, it's hard to stay focused on what really matters—helping the patients and their families." Recently Gina has begun saying prayers each day, not just for the patients but also for all the people who take care of the patients—the doctors, nurses, case managers, staff members, interns, hospital workers, family, friends, clergy, and visitors. She explains, "I began to sense that we need to reclaim this hospital not just as a business but primarily as a healing environment, a place where miracles can and do happen.

"When I say prayers each morning, I visualize the many ways that healing efforts are occurring all around me in this hospital. Each day the words are different, but I feel much stronger from talking with God and asking for support so that all of us can do the best work for the people who depend on us. Sometimes my prayers also focus on one or two individuals I've met in recent days who need an extra dose of divine strength and support. When I talk to God about a particular person who is ailing or battling for life, I usually picture this person's life force pulsing deep inside. I ask God to strengthen the pulse and the healing energies that operate within each cell of this person. I picture a ray of warm, golden light moving through this person's body, a light that emerges from the Divine Presence that exists in every human being. Sometimes I see that light going right to the place where this person is broken, and I plead with God, 'In Your great mercy, help this person return to wholeness. Help this person revive the loving and creative energies that You have placed in her soul. Help this person to be fully alive again.'"

To pray for someone who is ailing is one of the most inspiring things a human being is able to do. As these examples illustrate your moments of prayer can become some of the most intimate and important experiences of a lifetime. They allow you to look at the preciousness of life and search deeply for the energies of healing and wholeness that exist in each of our souls. I hope the prayers explored in this chapter and those that emerge from your own thoughts and feelings will deepen your connection to the Source of strength and compassion. I hope your quest for a return to wholeness will be met with divine mercy and profound success.

CHAPTER SIX

A Prayer for Breaking Free from a Habit That Hurts You or Others

Shivviti Adonai L-negdee tahmeed.	I place the Eternal before me always.

It's safe to assume that anyone who is reading this book has a fairly substantial level of intelligence. Yet no matter how smart we are, there are times in each of our lives when we feel somewhat out of control and we do unfortunate things. For example, we slip into old habits that we wish we didn't have.

One of the most beautiful teachings of Jewish spirituality is the ancient rabbinic discussion of how a person who struggles with imperfections and bad habits is superior in some ways to the person who finds it easy to be righteous. Jewish tradition recognizes that there is something noble and honorable about being imperfect and taking steps to overcome a trait or behavior that has been causing problems. The ancient words from the Talmud (a series of interpretations of the Bible and Jewish law) suggest: "There is an honored place where an individual who is transforming a personal failing can stand and where a thoroughly righteous individual is not entitled to stand."

As you may have discovered in your own life, part of being human is to have at least one bad habit that you know you ought to do something about, but it's hard to make that change. It could be a habit as complex as an addiction to alcohol, drugs, overeating, gambling, or volatile relationships that is draining your money or your health. Or it could be something as subtle as not listening when your spouse, your friend, or your child needs your undivided attention. It could be tending to be late and causing tension for yourself and others. It could be keeping silent when you ought to speak up or saying too much when you ought to guard your tongue. Or it could be being too trusting or too impulsive in relationships or in business, or assuming the worst about people who deserve a fair chance to prove they can come through.

Many of us have something we've known for years is hurtful to ourselves or to others, yet no matter how many times we put it on our New Year's resolutions or think about it in our Yom Kippur (Day of Atonement) prayers, it somehow remains. No matter how many times we feel embarrassed or frustrated about a certain undesirable trait or behavior, we can't seem to break free from it.

Looking Within

Do you know what your own troublesome habit might be? Do you have a sense of what less than perfect trait or behavior your soul is trying to work out during this lifetime? Look back at what you've been promising in your annual vows to God or in your private vows to the people in your daily life. What might be your most difficult trait or behavior? If you asked the men and women who've seen you in action, what might they say is the one habitual thing you do that is costing you, your loved ones, or your associates week after week, month after month? If you look back at the times when relationships or work projects fell apart, is there a recurring theme or pattern that you might want to explore?

One of the purposes of spirituality and psychotherapy is to give us skills for overcoming bad habits that we haven't been willing or able to resolve on our own. In psychology there has been significant progress in the past few decades for helping men and women outsmart even the most stubborn habits.

In Jewish spirituality, especially in the Mussar movement (teachings on exemplary conduct, developed in the nineteenth century by Rabbi Israel Salanter of Lithuania), Jewish prayer and study are carefully directed at identifying and transforming our shortcomings. In this tradition, which combines frequent, honest self-examination with spiritual teachings, each day is a new opportunity to write down our personal imperfections in a private notebook and seek ways to overcome them.

Anyone who has studied Jewish teachings in depth will notice that the entire calendar of sacred holidays and family rituals is filled with chances to examine and improve how we treat others and how we overcome our personal failings. Most rabbis and teachers recommend that the prayers written for each of the various holidays are not just for God's benefit but to open up our hearts and minds so we can become better people. The more you study the spiritual meaning underlying each of the major Jewish holidays, the more you will discover the personal growth themes inherent in each of these traditions.

Drawing from the best methods of both psychology and Jewish spirituality, this chapter will focus on an extremely powerful prayer and some additional types of support that can be used to snap out of self-defeating habits and unhealthy traits you may have wanted to change for a long time. *Please note* that I am not saying this prayer can replace other types of counseling and support. I still recommend that twelve-step programs, psychotherapy, an outstanding one-on-one mentor, or a good support group is crucial for making significant personal changes. But if you want to strengthen and boost your efforts to stop a bad habit or resolve a difficult trait, this prayer can help enormously as a supplement.

Admitting What Hasn't Worked

Before I get to these powerful methods for overcoming a bad habit, it's important to take note of what you've tried thus far. Many people are reluctant to engage in counseling or to use spiritual techniques *until all other avenues have been tried.* So let's examine what methods you may have already attempted for dealing with your most troublesome imperfection or shortcoming. Be honest as you answer the following questions:

Have you tried denial?

Most people spend at least a few days, months, or years in the much-visited State of Denial, saying things like "I don't have a problem," "It's not that serious," or "I've got it under control."

Have you tried blaming someone else for the problem?

Most people gain some temporary relief by saying the problem was caused or prolonged by someone else. Have you ever noticed yourself saying, "The reason I overeat is because you bring this fattening food into the house," "The reason I can't stop drinking is my boss is so impossible to work with," or "The reason I can't stop interrupting people is no one will let me speak."

Have you tried working on someone else's problem to take the attention off your own shortcomings?

This is a favorite technique especially of highly educated people and those in the helping professions. Have you ever noticed yourself giving advice or encouragement to a family member, friend, or client when you are secretly needing that very same advice or encouragement? Have you ever noticed that you're obsessing about someone else's imperfections and neglecting to do very much about your own?

Have you tried spending money and time on books, experts, and programs but not following through with their specific steps?

The majority of self-improvement books and tapes are put on a shelf and not followed. The majority of people who join diet programs and recovery programs do not sufficiently stick with the valuable steps, mentoring, and ongoing support provided by these programs. Finally, the majority of people who pay experts for advice tend to jump from one expert to another without fully utilizing what any expert suggested.

Does any of this sound familiar? If any of these descriptions sounds like you or someone you know, perhaps it's time to say, "We've tried the usual stalling techniques. Now let's get serious about following through on a combination of methods that can work day after day to break this harmful trait or behavior." If you are interested in trying something unusual but highly effective for boosting your efforts to break free from a bad habit, read on.

Utilizing a Powerful Mystical Phrase

In Judaism there is a meditation technique that has been practiced for centuries to help people go deeper in their prayers. It has also been used to overcome bad habits and self-sabotaging urges in order to refocus on what could be more life enhancing. The technique is to concentrate with all your heart and mind as you repeat a simple but mystically powerful phrase that comes directly from Psalm 16, verse 8. The Hebrew is *"Shivviti Adonai L-negdee tahmeed,"* and it usually gets repeated several times in both Hebrew and English. You can do it with your eyes open or closed.

In English this holy phrase can be translated as "I place the Eternal before me always." In some translations, such as the 1985 version issued by the Jewish Publication Society, this passage is translated, "I am mindful of the Presence of the Eternal. . . . I will not be shaken."

Consciously meditating on this phrase (almost like a Jewish mantra) to direct the mind away from harmful or distracting urges has been practiced in some Kabbalistic circles for several centuries. In addition, during the eighteenth and nineteenth centuries throughout Europe and North Africa (especially Morocco), a *shivviti* was utilized in many traditional congregations. On this carefully decorated card or tablet were the words *shivviti* (I set before me, I place before me, or I am mindful) and Yud-Hei-Vov-Hei (the unspeakable name of God, often referred to as Adonai but best translated as the Eternal One Who Is Forever Becoming).

Although I'd seen this *shivviti* card many times on the walls of certain synagogues, I had never actually concentrated on this mystical phrase until seven years ago, when I was at a spiritual retreat with one of my favorite teachers, Rabbi Ted Falcon of Seattle. Along with other activities that weekend over ninety participants spent several hours singing, praying, and meditating on the phrase "*Shivviti Adonai L-negdee tahmeed*—I place the Eternal before me always" to see how it lifted our minds off whatever was pulling on us.

I was surprised at how powerful the exercise was for me and for many others at the retreat. I had studied in psychology many types of thought stopping, relaxation, and mind control to help people who experience persistent difficulties with various urges they wish they didn't have. This ancient phrase from Psalm 16 struck me as a possibly useful tool that could deepen one's spiritual connectedness as well as help one break free from intrusive thoughts and urges. What if repeating this brief but inspiring ancient phrase could help people overcome negative habits? I was interested in learning more about it.

Changing an "Uncontrollable" Habit

A few weeks after I came back from the retreat, I was listening to a client tell me about a lingering habit he was having trouble resolving. Brad, a highly educated management consultant, confided that he had a longtime habit of staring "a little too long" at attractive women who passed by when he was with his wife or his teenage daughter at a restaurant, a movie, or some other family event. Brad felt embarrassed and a bit pessimistic about whether he could rid himself of this habit. He admitted, "I feel like a jerk for still having these wandering eyes. I know most men do this to some extent, but I'm happily married, and the last thing I want to do is upset my wife and my daughter by letting them see my head getting turned by one of these stunners. It's especially awkward if my eyes start wandering in the middle of a conversation—my wife saw me do this a few weeks ago and said, 'What am I, chopped liver?'"

When I asked Brad what he'd done so far to stop the habit, he told me, "I've tried lots of different ways to ignore the problem, rationalize the problem, or even write long lists of affirmations—saying that I will stop doing things that might make my wife, my daughter, or some stranger walking down the street feel uncomfortable. But each time I promise not to stare, I go back to being extra sneaky and hoping I won't get caught. It's embarrassing to be run by your hormones."

I asked Brad if he had ever considered spiritual approaches to his dilemma. He laughed for a moment and commented, "Do you mean imagining that God is going to strike me dead for having these lustful urges?"

I said, "No, that's not what I'm suggesting."

So we talked about his views of God and religion. Brad happened to be Jewish, but he had never been exposed to ideas about God beyond the angry, punitive version he'd picked up as a child from his authoritarian father. At one point he asked, "Is there some spiritual method in Judaism to deal with a problem of self-control like the one I'm having?"

That's when I offered a few ideas. First, I mentioned that the founder of the Chasidic movement, the Baal Shem Tov (the Master of the Good Name), had a two-step remedy for when an attractive individual catches your eye and distracts you from what you know in your heart you ought to be doing. The Baal Shem Tov recommended, "First, say a quick silent prayer of thanks to the Creator of the universe who has blessed this world with so much beauty. By remembering the ultimate Source of the beauty in front of you, you can raise up your awareness and break free of the distracting thoughts." You are consciously reminding yourself that the attractive person is not an object or a soulless body but rather a sensitive human being just like you with a spark of the divine deep inside that needs to be treated with dignity.

Second, the Baal Shem Tov would say to repeat a few times a refocusing statement such as *"Shivviti Adonai L-negdee tahmeed*—I place the Eternal before me always." That will help you to get back to your higher purpose in that moment.

Brad was surprised. "You mean it's not about feeling guilty? I always thought that religion was mostly about rules and guilt."

I told Brad that he wasn't alone. Many men and women throughout history have felt that religion can become too heavy with rules and guilt. Then I explained that in Judaism examining our shortcomings and getting support for making positive changes is a holy and cherished process, not a demeaning or shameful one. The Hebrew word *teshuvah*—to turn in a more positive or holy direction—refers to the daily, weekly, and yearly process of examining how to improve the way we treat others and ourselves *not because we are evil or bad people* but because we human beings need frequent reminders and support for bringing out our very best.

I told Brad, "There certainly are some Jewish teachings that are big on guilt, but most knowledgeable rabbis and sacred writings suggest that doing *teshuvah*—turning yourself around—is not about carrying a huge load of debilitating guilt or dreading that some external deity is going to punish you. It's more about reawakening the compassionate and healthy part of the soul that gets blocked or ignored in all of us from time to time. *Teshuvah* and personal renewal in Jewish spirituality are more about reconnecting with the sparks of goodness and light that we each carry inside us.

They're about deciding how you want to be God's partner in repairing the world and how you want people to be treated in this world that you're cocreating."

For the next few weeks Brad experimented with this two-step process for breaking free from visual distractions. He reported, "At first I kept finding ways to cheat. I'd say a prayer of thanks for the beauty of God's creation. I'd even repeat the *shivviti* phrase a few times. But I was still sneaking in an extralong glance and being run by my hormones. Nothing worked until I really began to think about what the *shivviti* phrase is saying. I had to seriously consider what it might mean if we truly are God's partners with the responsibility of cocreating a world where people get treated with decency. I had to stop and decide how I want my portion of the world to function."

Using the Shivviti prayer at least once a day with a clearer understanding of its deeper meaning, Brad began to make some progress. He reported after a few more weeks that he was almost 100 percent free from the habit. He told me, "For the first time since I was an adolescent, I feel a lot more in charge of the way I behave when I'm around an attractive woman. This sense of being a human partner working in tandem with a loving Divine Presence snapped me out of the obsession to keep staring. I've found I can appreciate someone's beauty for a quick second and immediately refocus on what God would want me to do—to be a *mensch* (a decent person) who treats each human being with respect and compassion."

How Does It Work?

I have found during the past seven years of testing out this Shivviti technique that it works at least 70 percent of the time to help people, including adults and teens who are in recovery programs or counseling for their strong urges for overeating, alcohol, drugs, gambling, or overspending. I've also seen the Shivviti prayer help men and women whose bad habits consist of being too trusting, too pessimistic, too impatient, too shy, prone to interrupting people, as well as other problems of impulsivity and hasty decision making in their love life or work life.

To understand why this ancient spiritual phrase works so well, we need to explore what happens physiologically and cognitively when people feel a strong urge to do something they know deep inside they shouldn't do. Consider this following illustration of how a mystical expression like *Shivviti* can help us in a practical way.

Imagine for a moment that a chocolate or sweets addict gets bored or feels anxious at 3 P.M. He or she usually experiences at that moment a depletion of serotonin and other pleasure-related chemicals in the brain. As soon as this person simply *imagines* getting a piece of Godiva chocolate or a serving of Häagen-Dazs ice cream, a rush of adrenaline and excitement surges through his or her body. You probably know from experience that if you indulge in some forbidden or unhealthy activity it tends to give you quick, temporary relief from your edgy feelings. But you also know that side effects, regrets, and sometimes feelings of shame ("Why do

I do this to myself?" "Why can't I break this bad habit?")
show up later.

This rush of adrenaline from imagining yourself getting
an unhealthy treat sends a message to the brain with a strong
sense of inevitability: "Hurry, I must have that forbidden
pleasure. Nothing else will do the trick." It's the same kind
of adrenaline rush and feeling of inevitability that an alco-
holic feels when he or she imagines self-medicating a feeling of boredom or anxiety with a stiff drink. Or the same
rush a shopaholic feels when imagining how good it's going
to feel to buy something to quell feelings of emptiness. Or
the same urgency a gambler feels when imagining how good
he or she will feel once the betting starts.

This cycle of reduced serotonin followed by an adrenaline rush while planning a way to acquire the forbidden treat
is described by many addicts and hasty decision makers as
"an uncontrollable urge." If at that moment you just try to
talk yourself out of the desire, your surging biochemistry
will probably overtake you and propel you further into an
adrenaline rush that seems to say, "I really must have that
forbidden treat to quell these cravings. I must do something
right now to calm these urges."

To stop a habit that has so much physiological urgency,
most people need to do more than just talk themselves out
of it, especially since we humans tend to dissociate at
moments like this—we actually tune out a part of our rational, decision-making brains. We feel we need a quick fix,
and we desperately have to do something about the adrenaline secretions racing through our bloodstreams that cause

such a strong feeling of inevitability. Since our biochemistry becomes extremely demanding at moments like these, most addicts and people with chronic habits report feeling "almost glad that the rational mind shuts off so that I can go do the thing I wouldn't otherwise do and I won't have to feel so conflicted about it. I'm glad I can just run away from myself [which psychologists call dissociation] at those moments."

To reverse this cycle of physiological adrenaline rush and psychological dissociation, it can be helpful to turn to a spiritual method. Quickly and carefully tuning in to the spiritual part of the mind breaks the adrenaline cycle and gives you some of the same physiological and psychological payoffs you would get from indulging in the forbidden or impulsive activity. Specifically, when you say a prayer of gratitude, when you stop to talk with God, or when you meditate quietly on your connection to a loving Source of strength and dignity, two things happen.

You receive your pleasure from a better source. If you take a few minutes to repeat slowly and mindfully the phrase *"Shivviti Adonai L-negdee tahmeed*—I place the Eternal before me always," you will experience a substantial but harmless (no side effects or addictive dependency) rush of serotonin and other pleasure chemicals. These good feelings are generated from inside your brain, and they can spread through your circulatory system to all the depleted zones of your body. Numerous research studies have shown that moments of intense prayer and feelings of deep gratitude to the Creator or the Divine Presence can produce a noticeable amount of pleasure chemicals in the brain, the circulatory system, and the entire nervous system.

By praying, meditating, or connecting with a loving Presence, you get your mind off the forbidden treat and onto a whole different kind of treat—feeling at one with a sacred flow of energy or being able to experience a profound closeness with God. If you repeatedly remind yourself to "place the Eternal before me always," you instruct your subconscious to let go of the unhealthy treat and focus instead on the satisfying spiritual connection.

You eventually begin to feel mastery over some habit that previously dominated your thoughts and actions. One of the greatest benefits of utilizing the Shivviti prayer (along with other types of support, such as having a mentor, a goals group, a twelve-step program, or some books that you can depend on during moments when you're tempted to slip back into old habits) *is that you get your life back.* Instead of using up lots of time figuring out how to sneak in some of your "guilty pleasures" and then feeling regret later, you now have a lot more energy available for doing things of greater purpose each day. Each time you say no to an unhealthy habit, it will give you a sense of personal mastery—you will no longer be a slave to your biochemical urges.

According to Jewish spiritual teachings, the most satisfying victory of your *teshuvah* (turning in a more positive or holy direction) is when you have a new opportunity to go back and do the bad habit but this time you reach out for support from people who care and from your connection to a Divine Presence. Instead of feeling regretful and defeated again, this time you feel connected to the creative life force that is working in all of us to improve this broken world and guide our fragile selves.

Are You Ready to Take Action on the Habit That Has Held You Back?

Now that you understand more about the biochemistry and the psychology of why habits are so hard to break, are you interested in taking the next step? Would you like to experiment with using an ancient spiritual phrase to overcome your most frustrating or unpleasant habit?

The next time you notice that you are almost ready to slip back into a negative behavior that is harmful to you or to someone else, realize this is your chance to try something different. Take a deep breath in and out as you say several times (to yourself if you are around other people or out loud if you are alone) these sacred words of connection to your higher purpose: "*Shivviti Adonai L-negdee tahmeed*—I place the Eternal before me always."

Then take a few moments to think about what these words mean to you. What would it be like if you could bring a sense of holiness into this situation where you feel susceptible to doing something you know you will regret later? What might happen if you checked in to the wisdom of your soul or the guidance you imagine God would give you at a moment like this? Instead of trying to run away from yourself or hide from your spiritual core, what would it be like to utilize all the parts of your mind and spirit in making this next decision? Asking these questions can profoundly change the way you act during moments of temptation—especially if you combine this spiritual work with the support of caring people who have struggled and been successful with a similar challenge.

For example, consider what happened to Evvy, a thirty-two-year-old counseling client of mine. Her story might inspire you or someone you know to have the courage to take steps to overcome even the most persistent and difficult habit.

"I Rediscovered a Part of Myself That I Had Buried Years Ago"

Evvy came for counseling because she felt stressed out from her job as an executive assistant at a high-pressure law firm. She explained during her initial session, "Each day there are so many things on my To Do list and so many prickly personalities I have to contend with. I wish I had the energy to do more things at night to nourish my soul, but after an extremely long day at the office all I can do when I get home is have a couple of glasses of wine, play a video game, eat some junky snacks, and collapse in bed with the TV on. That doesn't sound like the kind of life I thought I would be having now that I'm in my thirties, but that's about all I can handle these days."

When I asked Evvy which of these habits she might want to change, she hesitated and said cautiously, "I'm willing to explore how I handle the stress at work and maybe I'd be willing to cut back on the video games or the junky snacks. But that's all."

"Any chance we get to work on the two glasses of wine?" I asked, not sure if it was a significant concern for her.

Evvy looked at me with a worried expression. "Are you saying I have a drinking problem?" It was several weeks before Evvy was willing to look at the fact that ever since she had been in college she had been drinking two or three glasses of wine or beer each night to calm herself down. She admitted this to me during a session that came the day after she'd had a fight with her older sister, who accused her of being an "angry drunk."

Evvy's sister had told her, "Whenever we get together, it starts out pleasant because you have the most wonderful personality and the sharpest mind. But after you've put away two or three glasses of wine or beer, something changes. There's an ugly sarcasm and a snippiness about the way you talk when you're a little bit drunk. You say you're just feeling loose and free, but I'm willing to bet one of the reasons you've been having so much trouble in relationships is that you're starting to show signs of being an angry drunk."

Evvy was furious with her sister for being "so judgmental and uptight." But as we talked further about Evvy's usual ways of coping with stress, it became clear her sister was being fairly accurate. Evvy admitted that in each of her last three relationships, "Everything starts out fine, but if I'm stressed from work and I have a few drinks to unwind, I guess I do become somewhat sarcastic and snippy. One of my boyfriends told me, 'On a good day you're Glenn Close in *The Natural* or in *The Big Chill*. After a few drinks you're Glenn Close in *Fatal Attraction* or *101 Dalmatians.*'"

Over the next few weeks Evvy and I began to explore what kind of life she wanted to create for her early thirties and beyond. I wanted to hear what really mattered to her— what might be her higher purposes in life. During these brainstorming sessions Evvy described how she longed to be in a quality relationship, how she wanted to get involved in a once-a-week volunteer activity that made a difference in someone's life, and how she hoped to find a stronger sense of energy and satisfaction.

She commented, "I really believe there's got to be more to life than slogging through huge egos at work each day and then coming home so drained all I can do is run away from myself. If I don't make some changes soon, I'll end up ten years older and a whole lot more tired and frustrated than I am already."

What is most remarkable and important about Evvy's therapy is that she was honest and genuine about her hesitations. Evvy told me point-blank that she was terrified of seeking an alternative to her job. "Even though I hate the job and how it wears me down, I can't imagine taking the risk of trying something unknown." She also told me directly that she was extremely reluctant to give up her junky snacks, her video games, and her two or three drinks a night. She said, "Those guilty pleasures have become like a perfect companion each night when I come home tired and frustrated. I'm not looking forward to giving them up."

Evvy further admitted she had some reluctance about going to a twelve-step recovery group for food or alcohol because of the "Higher Power" terminology in those programs, which, she said, "makes me feel uncomfortable, like they're going to try to shove some religion down my throat."

I asked Evvy if she had ever felt comfortable praying or reading about spiritual issues. She was quiet for a moment, and I saw tears in her eyes. Then she told me, "When I was a young girl I felt very connected to God and to the spiritual beauty I sensed when I was in nature. But when my parents were getting divorced—I was twelve at the time—my world seemed to fall apart and I just stopped communicating with God or looking at life from a spiritual perspective."

I asked Evvy if she would be willing to use the Shivviti prayer the next time she felt empty inside or tempted to numb out with food or alcohol. At first she said, "I don't know if that's me. I think I'd feel self-conscious trying to get close to God again after all these years."

But a few weeks later she told me, "The other night I was absolutely exhausted from work, and I went to the refrigerator to get some ice cream sandwiches and a beer. Right as I opened the door of the fridge I stopped for a moment and imagined myself surrounded in sunlight—like when I was a little girl and I would take long walks on family vacations in Maine. I closed my eyes and said the words you suggested, '*Shivviti Adonai L'negdee tahmeed*—I place the Eternal before me always.' For the first time in years I felt that same warm connection to a mysterious but powerful Presence. I felt a renewed sense of inner strength, and I decided right then to close the refrigerator door and pour myself a tall glass of water instead. Then I sat down with a spiritual book one of my friends had given me six months ago that I hadn't opened yet. I read for almost an hour, and this sense of peace and calmness came over me. I felt like I had rediscovered a part of myself that I had buried when my parents were divorcing. It was like a sense of hope and a strong commitment to being fully alive that I had not experienced for a long, long time."

Because of her honesty and her willingness to look at and resolve each underlying fear and hesitation, Evvy was able to take the next steps and start exploring better options. After a few weeks of talking with placement firms, she found an excellent new job in a much saner and less stressful organization. She joined a twelve-step program to examine ways of cutting out snacks and alcohol that were, in her own words, "keeping me sedated and numb every night." She made two close friends in her recovery program, and one of them became a daily phone partner who helped her start each day with a positive plan and a lot of support. She also got fixed up by one of the women at her weekly volunteer involvement and began dating a man with whom she is currently having a good relationship.

While not every client has breakthroughs of this magnitude, Evvy worked hard day after day on overcoming her habits. Like a number of people who felt overwhelmed by loss or disruption in their lives, Evvy had shut down and sedated herself for a long time. Now she was coming back to life. If her story sounds like you or someone you know, I hope that either the Shivviti prayer or something else can reawaken this passion for living that we all have inside us.

In Your Own Words

Using prayer to assist other efforts to overcome a bad habit can take different forms for different people. Here are two examples of how people from all walks of life have used the Shivviti prayer in creative ways. Possibly their words will inspire you to compose a prayer of your own that can help stop a habit that has been in your life for too long.

The Interrupter

One of my clients was a powerful executive in his fifties who used the Shivviti prayer and a number of other techniques to overcome his longtime habit of interrupting his wife, his two children, and his business associates. He had come into therapy to find out why so many people had pulled away from him. We focused during several sessions on his habit of being too impatient and too controlling in many of his conversations, especially with the people he cared about most.

When I asked him to compose a prayer to help him change this costly habit, he wrote:

Shivviti Adonai L'negdee tahmeed.

Please, God, let me remember always to think about Your patience and Your kindness when I'm talking to people.

I can get so swept up in my own agendas and my own opinions that I forget there is a fragile soul in front of me who needs me to stop and listen.

I grew up with two parents who couldn't stop interrupting, so I know what it feels like to be dominated and squelched unfairly.

Please, God, help me to stop doing to my wife, my kids, and my associates what was done to me.

Please remind me somehow to stop and wait until they've had their say. Amen.

The Impulsive Decision Maker

Another of my clients was a female clothing designer in her forties who used the Shivviti prayer as part of her method for slowing down and not making hasty decisions in business or in personal relationships. Her prayer was

Shivviti Adonai L'negdee tahmeed.

May I always think about the Eternal One, who works in mysterious ways, and may I learn to let things unfold in their proper time.

May God's strength be with me as I stop myself from rushing into things that need time to develop.

May God's gentle caring be with me as I calm myself down so I can approach each new situation with wisdom and gracefulness. Amen.

Breaking Free

In this chapter you've been asked to consider what might be a bad habit that has been harmful to you or those who share your life. I realize it's not easy to face oneself or to make significant changes. But if any of the questions or examples in this chapter stirred thoughts about improving one area of your life that is less than it could be, I hope you will take a few moments to do something positive about it as soon as possible. You can use the exact words of the ancient Shivviti phrase ("*Shivviti Adonai L'negdee tahmeed*—I place the Eternal before me always"). Or you can write and say some heartfelt words of your own choosing to help you open up to a healthier way of being.

Please know that it's never a simple matter to change a longtime habit. It takes courage, persistence, support, and guidance. Saying a prayer and asking for help can assist you on your journey toward greater freedom and vitality. I hope that your efforts are successful and that one day you will look back and say, "That was quite a stubborn habit I worked hard day after day to overcome. But it definitely was worth the effort to make those changes."

CHAPTER SEVEN

A Prayer to Help You End the Day with Deeper Insights and Serenity

Hahsh-ki-veinu Adonai Eloheinu l'shalom	Help us, Eternal One, to lie down in peace,
V'ha-ahmideinu mahlkeinu l'khayim.	And to rise up, our Ruling Force, to life.
Uf'ros ahleinu sukkat sh'lomekha . . .	Spread over us the sheltered covering of your peace and wholeness . . .

Do you ever have trouble falling asleep (or falling back to sleep if you wake up in the middle of the night or too early in the morning)? Do your thoughts ever rush in and demand to be resolved even though you are trying to drift off to sleep? Does your body ever feel keyed up even though you're hoping to relax and unwind?

Researchers who specialize in sleep problems have come up with many explanations as to why more than 60 percent of adults currently have trouble falling asleep or getting enough sleep. It might be your thyroid, your brain's biochemistry, your hormones, your blood pressure, or the fact that you've eaten too much salt or spicy food.

In addition, for most people it's about something more than just physical factors. Forty years ago a number of psychologists and sociologists said we were living in the "Age of Anxiety." Today there seems to be something far more severe than anxiety keeping us up at night. Based on what I've observed in my counseling office and learned from talking to experts in the field, I would call this the "Age of Overload." Most people today describe their daily lives as being "way too busy," having "too much on my plate," or being "pulled in too many directions at once."

As one of my counseling clients told me recently, "Every day I feel torn from having to make tough choices that invariably let someone down. If I choose to work as hard as my job demands, then my family or my personal life suffers. If I take time off to be with the people I love, then my work piles up tremendously. At night when I put my head down on the pillow, I can't relax. All I can think about are the things I wasn't able to complete that day and the fact that I'm probably not going to have enough time to get them done tomorrow." Does this sound familiar to you? Is there a way to find a sense of wholeness and completion at the end of the day so that your body and your mind can relax?

Jewish spirituality has a suggestion. There's an ancient prayer to help overloaded men and women let go of the tension and regain a sense of well-being that allows them to sleep in peace and awaken the next day ready to be at their best. Based on the levels of stress and sleep-deprivation I see in most of the people I talk to these days, I would say we need this prayer more than ever.

The Bedtime Shema

Most Jewish children and adults are familiar with the first few words of the Shema prayer, especially the declaration "Hear, O Israel, Adonai is our God, Adonai is One." This statement of faith—which was first articulated by Moses when he was explaining the key principles of Judaism to the gathered multitude in the biblical Book of Deuteronomy (6:4–9)—is recited at nearly every prayer service. Usually spoken in a strong voice by the entire congregation, it is a declaration of belief that there is one unifying God (rather than many gods, as in certain other religions).

For some people the Shema is a declaration of Jewish identity. For others it's a reminder of all the men and women throughout history who recited the Shema as their final words before dying. Still others experience the Shema as a way to transcend the stressful material world in order to connect with the unity of a loving Presence.

Even Jews who don't know the difference between a tukhis and a tashlikh know how to recite the Shema. (In case these words are unfamiliar, you sit on your tukhis and you toss bread crumbs in a body of water at the Jewish New Year for tashlikh.)

Yet as familiar as most people are with the first few words of the Shema, more than 90 percent of Jews today have little or no experience with the extended Bedtime Shema, the traditional prayer of relaxation and peacefulness that you can say just before falling asleep at night. Even though this nighttime ritual has been a part of Jewish spirituality for almost two thousand years, in modern times it has rarely been taught to anyone except Orthodox students.

During fourteen years of Jewish education when I was growing up, I never heard anyone explain the significance of the Bedtime Shema. But in my adult years I have found this prayer can be extremely profound and useful both in my own life and for my clients. So don't be embarrassed if you've never studied or practiced the Bedtime Shema. You are certainly not alone.

Discovering a Healthy Spiritual Method for Deepening Your Sleep and Your Dreams

According to tradition, there are at least four steps to the Bedtime Shema ritual. A small percentage of people reading this book will quickly begin to practice not only these four steps but also some of the Psalms (91, 3, 128) and the hymn "Adon Olam," which are recommended to put your mind and body in a profound state of spiritual surrender at bedtime. However, for most readers I would recommend taking it slowly. According to Yitzhak Buxbaum, author of the book *Jewish Spiritual Practices,* "It is best when you begin this practice to do it for, let us say, five minutes. It is a general rule when you begin new spiritual practices not to overburden yourself. Once it becomes habitual and easy you can then lengthen the time according to your desire."

My goal is not to *add* to your nighttime stresses by giving you a list of requirements or demands. Rather, I offer you four specific steps for reducing tensions and increasing spirituality as you enter the world of sleep and dreams. Each of the four steps is remarkable on its own. Whatever portion of the Bedtime Shema ritual you practice will enrich your life and deepen your sense of health and inner wisdom.

On a technical note, there are many ways to say the Bedtime Shema. Some people read the prayers in bed with a flashlight that has a push-button release mechanism that turns off when they drift into sleep. Others read the prayers with a light on, then turn the light off before saying a few final personal thoughts to God. Still others improvise on the themes of the Bedtime Shema (which I will describe) and do the entire ritual in the dark. As you become more familiar with the four sections of the Bedtime Shema, you will probably develop a style of your own.

The First Step: Letting Go of the Frustrations You Don't Need to Carry into Your Bed

In most traditional prayer books the first part of the Bedtime Shema is as follows. (Note: I am including only the first line of the Hebrew along with the entire English translation. If you want the complete Hebrew prayer, it can be found in many prayer books, including *The Complete Artscroll Siddur.*) Here are the initial words that are intended to give relief to your mind and body:

Ribono shel olam, hahreinee mokheil l'khal mi sheh-hikh-ees v'hikneet ohtee, oh shekhatah c'negdee.

Master of the universe, I hereby forgive anyone who an-
gered or antagonized me or who sinned against me—
whether against my body, my property, my honor or
against anything of mine; whether this person did so
accidentally, willfully, carelessly, or purposely; whether
through speech, deed, thought, or notion; whether in
this lifetime or another lifetime—I forgive every child of
God. May no person be punished because of me. May it
be your will, Eternal One, my God and the God of my
ancestors, that I may sin no more. Whatever sins I have
done before You, may You blot out in Your abundant
mercies, but not through suffering or bad illnesses. May
the expressions of my mouth and the thoughts of my
heart find favor before you, Eternal One, my Rock and
my Redeemer.

The question arises, How do you do this? How do you
forgive someone when you still feel resentful, frustrated, or
hurt? What if you don't feel ready yet to forgive or you
notice you're having bitter conversations with this person in
your mind? And how do you ask for God to remove your
sins (which in Hebrew refers to the times when you've
missed the mark or broken a vow)? What if you're still feeling
ashamed or guilty for something you did that was hurtful to
yourself or others?

The ancient rabbis were psychologically astute; they
realized that if you carry your bitterness or anger (toward
yourself or others) into bed with you, your sleep and your
dreams will be disrupted. Long before there were scientific

studies of REM (rapid eye movement dream states), the rabbis knew that we human beings need undisturbed sleep and healing dreams to be at our best. They suggested that each of our souls needs to drift into the wisdom and nourishment that dreams and deep sleep can provide; otherwise we will be stuck in our painful feelings about the unfinished business from the day.

The rabbis who put together the sequence of phrases in the Bedtime Shema knew that if you want to go to sleep with a sense of completeness and let your dreams take you to a place of transcendent wisdom and healing, it helps to understand the true meaning of forgiving yourself or others. Most people make the mistake of thinking forgiveness means declaring the guilty party innocent, whitewashing what was done, or pretending it never happened. These "forgive and forget" types of denial are *not* the true definition of forgiveness, either from a Jewish spiritual standpoint or even from most dictionaries.

If you look up the word *forgive* in Webster's dictionary or *The Oxford English Dictionary*, you will find it means "to give up resentment," "to pardon the person who committed an offense," "to cease to harbor bad feelings," "to give up claim to a payment or requital," and "to give up the need for revenge." Notice they don't say to whitewash, to forget, to pretend nothing happened, or to let this person do this same thing again.

Forgiving (as opposed to forgetting) starts with a genuine offender you cannot control and focuses instead on the need to make sure this offender doesn't leave you feeling resentful, stuck, or incomplete. It's more about your own feelings. Do you want to carry this grudge and estrangement any longer? Or do you want to let go of the bitterness so you can move on to something constructive? Do you want to keep having to be this person's secret jailer or judge? Or do you want to let go of the resentment so that you can open up to what can be learned or improved from this situation?

In counseling sessions I've often asked people, "Is it possible to see the person who did this terrible action as a wounded soul who needs help?" If you look at the offender not as a monster but as a child of God who needs help and guidance, your emotions begin to shift. Quite often you can then start to brainstorm about what might assist this person not to repeat the same hurtful actions. What would help the perpetrator stop next time? What would help you, the one who was mistreated, to recover and prevent having something like this done to you again? The resentment begins to go away when you realize that our true mission in life is to respond to painful events by asking not How do I get back at this person? but rather How do I make sure we don't keep repeating these same painful situations?

It may surprise you to find out that in Judaism forgiveness is a duty—even when the other person is clearly wrong. The Talmud says, "The quality of forgiveness is one of the finest gifts God bestowed on our ancestor Abraham and his seed . . . and it means forgiving before someone has even asked for forgiveness." In Rabbi David Cooper's book *God Is a Verb*, forgiveness in the Kabbalistic tradition is described as God's most excellent gift for each of us to utilize. Rabbi

Cooper explains that, "for the Kabbalist, forgiveness does not mean we need to embrace someone who has done a despicable act against humanity. Rather, it is focused on the degree to which we hold on to our anger or our negative feelings."

In Jewish teachings there are at least three ways to look at the benefits of forgiving and the costs of holding on to resentments.

It's not good for your body or your mind to become too rigid. The Hebrew word for forgiveness, *mokheil,* which you will find in the first sentence of the prayer in this section, means not only "to forgive," but also "to forgo, to get beyond." It has the same Hebrew root letters as *makhal,* which can mean "illness" or "disease" (and that's what can result if you get stuck in resentment or if your bitter feelings disrupt your sleep and your dreams). The Talmud says that a person who has been wronged should be pliant as a reed, not hard like the cedar. There are also many biblical and Talmudic passages about the need to forgive even the most painful mistreatment—not to whitewash what the person has done *but to forgive so that your own heart won't become hardened to people and life in general.*

As a psychologist I can verify that these teachings on forgiveness make a lot of sense. If an upsetting incident causes you to become rigid, inflexible, or unforgiving, it almost always can lead to physical and emotional symptoms. The incident is long over, yet the rigidity and bitterness continue to affect the way you act in all sorts of similar situations.

Rather than let your body tense up and your mind obsess on ways to get back at someone, you should focus on healing your own brokenness so that this painful incident doesn't scar you or hold you back for the rest of your life. There is a lot of useful wisdom in the prayer's request to "forgive every child of God. May no person be punished because of me."

In Jewish teachings becoming more forgiving allows you to give rebuke and constructive suggestions with a more compassionate attitude. In Chapter 3 we discussed the Jewish teachings on giving rebuke or constructive feedback to someone who has wronged or upset you. If you want the other person to hear what you're saying and to consider the merit of your suggestions, you first need to let go of your rage and self-righteousness. Once again, forgiveness doesn't mean whitewashing or ignoring what an offender has done. It means letting go of the need for revenge so you can do something to make things better for the future. Picturing yourself forgiving each wounded soul who has wronged you that day strengthens the part of your mind that is creative and compassionate. This will probably help you have a clearer perspective on what happened.

In Jewish spirituality you also can pray for God to assist you and this person to prevent additional incidents. Many rabbis and teachings suggest that as soon as you say this first section of the prayer, you write down briefly (on a piece of paper next to your bed, or in a notebook that you keep on your nightstand) ideas you have about how to improve the situation that caused the painful incident. Putting your ideas on paper is an extremely effective way of assuring yourself that you don't need to hold on to them when you're trying to fall asleep.

In essence this first step of the Bedtime Shema allows you to put in a safe place the angry emotions and churning thoughts you have about your day. Your brain will feel less burdened as you drift off to sleep if you set aside a few moments for letting go of resentments and putting in writing your suggestions about what should happen next to improve things. Especially if you are the kind of person who ruminates about unfinished emotional business when you're trying to fall asleep, or if you tend to have conversations in your head with the people who are most frustrating you, this step is very helpful.

For example, Gayle is a highly successful marketing executive and counseling client. She told me during her initial session, "On many nights when I need to be sleeping, I find myself having upsetting conversations in my mind with my advice-giving mother or my condescending older brother. Or it might be a dispute I'm trying to work out with my very controlling boss or my extremely dishonest ex-husband. There are way too many people who show up uninvited when I'm trying to fall asleep."

When Gayle first looked at the forgiveness prayer, she laughed and said, "Yeah, right! Like I want to rush out and forgive these people who have been so difficult. You gotta be kidding." However, when we discussed the fact that forgiveness doesn't mean whitewashing or giving in but rather freeing up Gayle's mind for constructive action and emotional relief, she became a little more interested. Over the next few weeks she experimented with saying this forgiveness prayer to unhook from each day's battles and writing down any ideas she would initiate the next day to improve how she dealt with her mom, her brother, her boss, or her ex-husband.

Gradually, Gayle found, "This forgiveness portion of the Bedtime Shema is pretty amazing. It's given me a sense of control and mastery each night. I can't change the basic personalities of the people who get on my nerves each day, but I can change how I react to them. Instead of staying stuck in bitterness and frustration, I've decided to forgive them for being who they are, and I try to focus instead on how to become more creative and effective in the way I deal with them. Not only has my sleep improved but I'm a lot less reactive and far more centered now when difficult people give me trouble."

Is there someone in your life who you need to forgive in order to regain your peace of mind? Is there a conflict that shows up in your thoughts when you are trying to fall asleep, or that enters your dreams? I know this is a difficult issue for many people, but if the first of the Bedtime Shema prayers can help you get beyond your angry feelings, then your sleep, your health, and your creativity will benefit significantly.

The Second Step: Asking for Assistance as You Prepare to Enter the World of Sleep and Dreams

In some prayer books the declaration *"Shema Yisra-el . . ."* comes next. But in most prayer books the guidelines of Maimonides, the twelfth-century philosopher, physician, and biblical scholar, are followed. His recommended second step of the Bedtime Shema is to ask for God's help in preparing the mind and body for a deeply peaceful and insightful night of sleep. Here are the first few Hebrew words and the entire English translation for this step:

> *Ba-rookh Atah Adonai Eloheinu melekh ha-olam, ha-mapil khev-lei shei-nah ahl ei-nai oot'noomah ahl ahf-pai.*

> Blessed are You, Eternal One, our God, ruling force of the universe, Who lowers down the bonds of sleep upon my eyes and slumber upon my eyelids. May it be Your will, Eternal One, my God and God of my ancestors, that You lay me down to sleep in peace and raise me upright tomorrow in peace. May my ideas, bad dreams, and bad notions not confound me; may my offspring be blessed with wholeness and completeness by You; and may You illuminate my eyes again tomorrow lest I die in sleep, for it is You Who creates light within the opening of my eyes. Blessed are You, Eternal One, Who illuminates the entire world with Your glorious Presence.

Many people call this second section of the Bedtime Shema the Ha-mapil prayer because of the phrase in the first sentence, "*Ha-mapil* (to lower down) *khev-lei* (the bonds or strands of) *shei-nah* (sleep)." This is a comforting and profound description of a loving Presence wrapping your eyes and your soul in an invisible protective web of sleep and dreams that connects you with holy wisdom and peace.

Most people who have said this part of the Bedtime Shema night after night find it much easier than the first step. You are asking the holy energies within you and around you to help you fall asleep tonight and wake up the next day successfully, as well as to have good dreams that aren't plagued by nightmares or disturbing images. It's as though you are alerting your unconscious mind that sleep and dreams are precious gifts from a holy Source and that you will need support and guidance throughout the night.

Some rabbis and spiritual teachers also recommend asking God to help you answer a specific question during your dreams, or to assist you with some type of holy guidance and clarity. The traditional practice is to say the Ha-mapil prayer and then ask God for help on a specific question or concern. I have seen many men and women successfully use this traditional request for assistance. There's no guarantee, but in many cases asking for guidance before you drift off to sleep will increase your likelihood not only of having a helpful dream but also of remembering it. You are essentially programming your subconscious mind to look for guidance on a topic and to wake up the next morning with some information from a mysterious Source.

I have had several wonderful experiences using this prayer for guidance. Several years ago I went through a frustrating period of sixteen months with a writing project that kept getting stalled. One night after saying the Ha-mapil prayer I asked for God's guidance on what I should do next about this project.

In the morning I woke up with an unusually clear recollection of a fascinating dream that seemed to be saying I should be writing and speaking not about the topic of the stalled project but rather about prayer. At first I was somewhat hesitant to set aside the project in which I had invested so much time and effort. I was nervous about focusing on prayer—what if no one was interested, or I wasn't the right person to be writing on such an important topic? Sometimes it's hard to know what a dream is telling us to do, and quite often a dream can have more than one interpretation.

But deep inside I had a strong sense that this dream was directly responding to my request for guidance. Even if it meant I needed to work through some substantial fears and hesitations, I knew I had to listen to what seemed to be a positive answer to my question. I decided that day to begin writing the book you are holding in your hands. I'm very glad that prayer and that dream helped me find this direction.

Think about your own life's journey and your desires and struggles. Is there a question about which you would like to receive some dream guidance? If you could ask God or the still small voice deep inside you for wisdom about an issue on which you have been unclear in your waking life, what might it be? Try asking for assistance on this issue after you say the prayer requesting God's help in protecting your mind and body during sleep.

The Third Step: Making a Connection to the One Whose Essence Is Love

Now we come to the pinnacle of the Bedtime Shema. This third section gives you the opportunity to truly let go and give up control so that your body and mind can drift into sleep and dreams.

For many people this isn't easy. All day long we try to control things, arrange things, and fix things. Then when we put our heads down on our pillows, we somehow are supposed to switch gears and let go of control. But what if your brain won't take a break from thinking, worrying, and planning? As you probably know from experience, *you can't force yourself to fall asleep.* You can only let go and allow sleep to come over you.

Jewish spirituality offers this third section of the Bedtime Shema as a way to stop being in charge and let something else—a mysterious loving Presence—take over while you rest. If these words ("let something else take over") seem strange or uncomfortable to you, please be patient. You might feel differently after you hear the complete explanation of how this process of spiritual relaxation works.

"Turning It Over to God"

The third section of the Bedtime Shema begins with three words, *"Eil melekh neh-ehmahn,"* calling upon "God, the trustworthy ruling force." In the words of a friend of mine, this is the moment when you "let go and let God," or when you close your eyes and say, "Whatever is left over and unresolved from the day, I turn it over to God for the night so I can sleep."

Some people can do this without difficulty. They have a strong sense of connection to a reliable and compassionate Divine Presence. So at bedtime or in the middle of the night when fears or concerns emerge, they can say, "I turn this over to God" and it feels reassuring to them.

Yet for many people, especially those who are skeptical about spiritual issues, "letting go and letting God" is not so easy. It might be that you're not quite ready to let go of your unresolved concerns or that you're not sure whether there is a trustworthy ruling force on which to rely. I recommend to counseling clients who have trouble relaxing or letting go of their worries at bedtime a quick exercise that you can try right now.

Stop for a moment and notice your breathing. Pay attention to how your breath flows in and moves out even when you aren't thinking about it or directing it. Surely some life force or energy is keeping you alive and helping you breathe even when your mind is on other things. Can you trust that life force? Can you surrender to it and know that it will keep your breath going in and out reliably and dependably? Can you feel pretty sure that even as you sleep this invisible life force will regulate your breath?

Jewish spirituality suggests that another way of describing this abundant life force, which helps you breathe even when you are sleeping, is "God, the trustworthy ruling force." When you close your eyes tonight, imagine yourself turning over responsibility for your breathing to this supportive life force, this Divine Presence. Even if you're unsure about how to describe God, you might have a sense that some benevolent force or energy is assisting your breathing process and protecting your soul.

Connecting to the Source of Love

The next six words of the third section of the Bedtime Shema are "*Shema Yisra-el Adonai Eloheinu, Adonai Ekhad,*" which are about listening and connecting with this life force and letting it fill you with a sense of Oneness and unity.

I have heard dozens of translations of these sacred words and hundreds of fascinating interpretations. This is one of the shortest but also one of the most profound prayers in Jewish spirituality. One of my favorite translations is the following (which I recommend you say slowly whenever you feel the desire to connect with God's caring Presence, including when you are drifting off to sleep):

Shema	Listen and understand
Yisra-el	you who strive with God.
Adonai	There is an Eternal Presence whose essence is love
Eloheinu	that is our God.
Adonai	This Eternal Presence whose essence is love
Ekhad	is One, Unified, Connected, Everywhere.

Let's be honest: Are you able to imagine yourself connecting with an Eternal Presence that expresses continually in our lives and that connects everything in the universe? Can you imagine yourself filled with the energy of Adonai (the infinite One Who is and will always be)? I realize these are huge spiritual questions, but they draw us closer to the deeper meaning of the "Shema Yisra-el" prayer. Instead of saying the "Shema Yisra-el" as an empty repetition of vague words, try saying it at least once a night just before falling asleep as a vehicle for connecting with the One that unifies the entire universe and that expresses through each of us.

For those who are skeptical about the existence of a loving God, this declaration can seem confusing or uncomfortable. To help you glimpse what these words mean on a practical level, *recall for a moment a time in your life when you felt deeply in love.* Do you remember being so filled with love that you felt intimately connected to everything that you sensed was alive and beautiful? At that moment you may have noticed how music sounded richer than ever, or that a walk in nature seemed more vibrant, or that you had a sense of eternity you'd never experienced as strongly before.

You may have wondered, "Where does this love come from? What is the source of this incredibly strong feeling?" If you were able to believe in love as a real but invisible life force, could you also imagine an extensive force or energy that expresses through each of us just like love does? This extensive force or energy is what many call God. You might disagree, but many people believe that when an atheist or skeptic speaks of love and when a spiritual person speaks to the Source of love, they are addressing the same energy. Whether you call this energy God or "the mysterious energy of love," Jewish teachings say they are one and the same.

Now it's up to you to try out this mystical process of spiritual connection at bedtime. If you say the "Shema Yisra-el" declaration slowly a few times and let yourself imagine a mysterious Source of love, which protects your soul even as you sleep, this sacred prayer can begin to transform any tensions or frustrations that are still lingering from your hectic day. Letting yourself be filled up with a feeling of love and completeness at bedtime is a good way to find a peaceful night's rest.

A Huge Relief

The next six words of the third section of the Bedtime Shema prayer are *"Barookh Sheim c'vohd, mahl-khootoh l'olam vah'ed."* One of the many ways to translate this ancient phrase is the following:

Barookh	Blessed is
Sheim	The Holy Name of God,
c'vohd	Whose glory and honor
mahl-khootoh	are powerfully manifested
l'olam	in this world
vah'ed	for all eternity.

When you say these words, "Blessed is the Holy Name of God, Whose glory and honor are powerfully manifested in this world for all eternity," you are connecting with a vast power source that is bigger than your individual mind and body. Feeling connected to this Source means you don't need to be in charge at night, and it allows you to let go even more deeply as you move closer to falling asleep.

For many people the idea that they don't have to be in charge at night is a huge relief. You spend much of your day trying to respond to all the challenges and responsibilities in your life. But at night, when you lie down in bed, you definitely can let something else be in charge—namely the mysterious One Whose energies are reflected in the beauty of nature and the power of ongoing creation. As you say the words *"Shema Yisra-el Adonai Eloheinu Adonai Ekhad"* and *"Barookh Sheim c'vohd mahl-khootoh l'olam vah'ed,"* imagine that you are letting go of your separateness and allowing your body to merge for the rest of the night with the unseen Eternal Presence that embraces all.

Feeling Embraced by the One Who Loves You

Quickly following the "Shema Yisra-el" and "Barookh Sheim" statements, the next several words of the Bedtime Shema are the guidelines from Deuteronomy 6, the V'ahavtah (which in English means "and you will love"). It's a brief prayer to help us remember to stop every so often during the day and reconnect with God or a loving Presence. Essentially, the V'ahavtah portion of the Bedtime Shema can be experienced as a promise you make to yourself to love and stay connected with the One who loves you.

Rabbi Debra Orenstein, who coauthored the books *Lifecycles*, volumes 1 and 2, recently offered a beautiful interpretation of the V'ahavtah prayer as the words we say to express the love we feel in response to a God Who expresses lovingly in our lives. Rabbi Orenstein commented, "I often hear from Jewish men and women of various ages and backgrounds that they've gone to numerous services for many years and they've never heard a rabbi say, 'God loves you.' Yet here in the Shema and the V'ahavtah, the implication is quite clear: 'Listen Israel, since there is a God who lovingly creates everything—including your soul, your life force, and all the beauty in your world—then you will of course want to love this caring God.' I am a rabbi who is pleased to let you know that yes, God loves you."

For many people this is a difficult concept to accept. You might be asking, "Does God really love an individual? Is that a myth, or is that something on which we can rely?" In Jewish spirituality you are asked to look at the evidence—you have been given the gift of life, the beauty of nature, the joy of learning, the opportunity to love and be loved, and the strength to deal with life's suffering and losses. Certainly if you take note of how abundant and remarkable this creation is, you will want to express some gratitude and love for the creative Source that keeps it all going. That's what the V'ahavtah ("and you will love") prayer allows you to do—to stay conscious and appreciative of the One that keeps it all going, that expresses lovingly in this world, even emerging through each cell of your body.

Here are the words of the V'ahavtah prayer that come next in the Bedtime Shema. Even if you've said these words hundreds of times previously, think about them as though saying them for the first time:

V'ahavtah eit Adonai Elohei-kha, b'khol l'vahv'v'kha, oov'khol nahf'shikha, oov'khol m'ohdekha.

And you will love the Eternal One, your God, with all your heart, with all your soul, and with all your resources. Let these matters guide you and be upon your heart. Teach them thoroughly to your children, and speak of them when you sit in your home, when you walk on the way, when you retire at night, and when you arise in the morning. Bind them as a sign upon your arm, and let them be reminders between your eyes. And write them on the doorposts of your house and upon your gates.

These often-repeated prayers—the "Shema Yisra-el" ("Listen and understand"), the "Barookh Sheim" ("Blessed is the Holy Name of God"), and the V'ahavtah ("And you will love")—are about letting yourself experience a loving connection between you and the Source of life. Since life is so precious and since the gift of life comes from a loving and creative energy force that is called God, these lines are a reminder not to take any of this for granted. As you move closer to falling asleep, you are reminding yourself that you live within the embrace of a source of love that we human beings can easily forget if we don't set up frequent reminders in our homes, on the paths we walk, or in the words we say when we go to sleep and when we wake up.

The intention of this third step of the Bedtime Shema is to let you enter the world of sleep and dreams not from an anxious state of mind because of your daily worries, but from a sense of being filled with spiritual love and connection. Instead of feeling fragmented or incomplete day after day, you can experience the fullness of being a holy spark of light in a remarkable spiritual universe.

The Fourth Step: Drifting into Sleep and Dreams with a Sense of Protection

Finally, with your eyelids heavy and your worries set aside, you are ready to float to a different kind of reality. But first there is one more prayer that can give you an additional sense of protection and support as you let yourself drift into sleep and dreams. Here are the words:

Hahsh-kiveinu Adonai Eloheinu l'shalom, v'hah-ahmideinu mahl'keinu l'khayim. Ufrohs ahleinu sukkaht sh'lomeh-kha.

Lay us down to sleep in peace, Eternal One our God, and raise us up, our protecting force, to life. Spread over us the shelter of Your peace. Set us aright with good counsel from Your Presence, and save us so that we may continue to serve You. Shield us, remove from us any foe, plague, sword, famine, and woe, and remove any spiritual blocks or impediments from in front of us and behind us and from inside us. And in the shadow of Your wings shelter us. God, You are the One Who protects us and rescues us. Our God, You are the gracious and compassionate ruling force. Safeguard our going and coming—for life and peace from now to eternity.

While this entire prayer is meant to be comforting and connecting, I want to alert you to the particular phrase that I have found most helpful in reducing anxiety and helping people enter the world of sleep and dreams with a sense of completeness rather than fragmentation. The phrase is *"Ufrohs ahleinu sukkaht sh'lomeh-kha,"* which usually gets translated "Spread over us the shelter of Your peace." It can also mean, "Surround us and fill us with your wholeness and completeness."

We human beings get fragmented and stressed quite often. Especially after a hectic day or on a night when your thoughts are racing through your head, it's easy to forget that we are spiritual beings connected to the whole of the universe, to the One who is complete. But if you say, *"Ufrohs ahleinu sukkaht sh'lomeh-kha*—Surround us and fill us with your wholeness and completeness," you may be able to feel yourself nourished and protected in a way you have never experienced before. Even if it takes a leap of faith to reach this state of relaxed surrender, I hope you will give yourself that gift and let yourself experience a deeper level of sleep and replenishment.

In Your Own Words

Since the Bedtime Shema is quite lengthy, many people shorten and personalize it in various ways. Here are a few possibilities to give you ideas for your own nighttime prayers.

One of my counseling clients, a rabbi with a strong interest in psychology, prepares for sleep by reading a portion of the traditional Bedtime Shema prayers and then talking with God about his unresolved issues from each busy day. If there are any resentments toward others or frustrations with his own actions that day, he writes in a notebook that he keeps on his nightstand about what he plans to do in the next few days to work through these issues. Then he turns off the light, and as he drifts off to sleep he says the "Shema Yisra-el" declaration three to seven times, slowly and mindfully.

As he told me recently, "It often relaxes me and helps me reach a very calm and peaceful state when I imagine letting go of my ego and letting God be in charge. Sometimes it's not easy to surrender like this, but if I sincerely want to be God's partner in repairing the world, I need to let God take over sometimes and not try to control everything myself."

Another of my counseling clients is a woman who says only the one sentence of the "Shema Yisra-el" declaration, then imagines herself floating into the gentle, invisible strands of love that she associates with the Shekhinah, the Divine Presence. She explains, "I grew up with a somewhat cold and distant mother, as well as an unavailable father. When I close my eyes and imagine myself embraced by the loving and connecting energies of the Shekhinah, it nourishes my soul in a profound way."

Yet another of my counseling clients is a poet who writes down in a journal each night her unfinished business, regrets and resentments from the day, as well as one question for which she wants some guidance from her dreams. Then she sets these notes aside as she closes her eyes and recites the words of the "Shema Yisra-el," followed by a personal prayer to God.

Recently, when she was feeling quite keyed up and over-loaded from an extremely frustrating day, she spontaneously spoke this personalized version of the Bedtime Shema, and it helped her let go and drift off to sleep.

Please, dear God,
let me forgive each person who didn't give me
what I thought I wanted this day.
And let me forgive myself
for being somewhat imperfect and overextended today as
    well.
Generous and abundant Creator,
I long to feel Your protection and Your love.
I'm learning to let You be in charge,
but I have difficulty at times letting go of control and
    trusting You.
Please guide my soul as I enter the nighttime world
of dreams and visions.
May I be assisted there
by Your holy wisdom and Your abundant peace.
Amen.

Each of us has a slightly different bedtime ritual. As you explore the various parts of the Bedtime Shema, see which phrases assist you in finding a sense of peace and release on a stressful night. Try out some or all of the sections of the Bedtime Shema to see which words and ideas comfort you when your mind is racing. And if you should wake up in the middle of the night with fears or agitation, let the words of these prayers relax your body and invite your consciousness to drift slowly into the world of dreams and renewal.

Conclusion

In each of the preceding seven chapters, my hope has been that you will find the unique words of prayer that touch your heart and soul. As I've stated throughout this book, Jewish prayer is not a fixed or rigid system but rather a constantly evolving process that invites us to offer up our personalized prayers. Whether you are praying for healing, for clarity of mind, or for improved personal effectiveness, I hope you will always dig deeply inside to find your truth and speak it with sincerity.

I believe that one of the purposes of prayer is to give us strength and focus to do good things in the world. I urge you to keep sharing your spirituality in gentle ways and making sure you do whatever you can to help repair the broken and painful situations in this world that call out for your assistance. I hope that this book assists you on your journey and that you will be able to share your gifts and your caring with many people, both those you have already met and those you will meet in the future. May the blessings of the Eternal One continue to express through you and your actions. Amen.

Recent Research Findings About Prayer

In the introduction to this book, I mentioned that there are over two hundred scientific studies from the past twenty years on how prayer can assist us in improving our physical health, our mental health, and our ability to cope with life's challenges. Here's a brief sample of these studies:

Prayer as a Way of Reducing Physical Pain and Discomfort

At the Arthritis Center of Scripps Clinic in San Diego, California, Drs. Terry Cronan, Robert Kaplan, Linda Posner, Elaine Blumberg, and Franklin Kozin did a study published in *Arthritis and Rheumatism* (vol. 32, no. 12, December 1989, pp. 1604–7). The team kept track of 382 people with painful musculoskeletal disorders, including severe arthritis. They charted each patient to see what nontraditional remedies had worked most effectively over a six-month period for reducing pain and increasing mobility and daily functioning. They found that 44 percent had used prayer during the past six months and 54 percent of those found it "very helpful," ranking prayer higher than dietary changes, vitamins, bed rest, swimming, exercise, massage therapy, and relaxation therapy. Bear in mind that these were not devout monks trained to use prayer and meditation to enter deep states of consciousness that could bypass pain receptors. These were everyday men and women with arthritis in a major American city.

These results are similar to what Jon Kabat-Zinn has found in his work at the University of Massachusetts Medical Center near Boston. As described in his book *Full Catastrophe Living* (New York: Delacorte, 1990) and reported in the article "The Clinical Use of Mindfulness Meditation for the Self-Regulation of Chronic Pain" (*Journal of Behavioral Medicine*, vol. 8, 1986, pp. 163–90), everyday men and women can be trained to use prayer and meditation to reduce significantly even the most severe chronic pain. People with chronic back problems, nerve disorders, traumatic injuries, recurring pain, and other ailments made remarkable progress in using prayer and meditation to regain their ability to live more fully.

Prayer as a Way of Improving How You Respond to What Life Presents You

At Duke University Medical School in Durham, North Carolina, Dr. Harold Koenig does research and teaching in psychiatry and internal medicine. In the May 24, 1995, issue of *JAMA: The Journal of the American Medical Association* (vol. 273, no. 20, pp. 1561–62), Dr. Koenig's findings on prayer as a way to improve recovery and coping mechanisms were discussed. His series of studies suggest that, "despite the presence of chronic disabling disorders (such as heart disease and diabetes), *people are less likely to become depressed if they score high in religious coping.*" He defines "religious coping" as "the use of religion to adapt to stress, including prayer, faith in God, and spiritual readings."

Dr. Koenig went on, "One of the strongest predictors of depression is disability. In our study, we showed that those with the most severe disabilities, such as heart disease or diabetes, and who scored high in religious coping, were less likely to become depressed compared with those who scored low in religious coping." His studies discovered, "There is an inverse relationship between religious coping and depression that was strongest among the most disabled persons. It did not necessarily prevent the disability, but it did prevent or reduce the depression that accompanies disability." In follow-up studies he found, "There seems to be a dynamic effect—in a six-month follow-up study of two hundred people, those who scored high in religious coping suffered less depression." Dr. Koenig concluded, "This finding is probably more important because over time those who were good religious copers became *less depressed.*"

Prayer as a Way of Moderating Heart Rate and Blood Pressure

Dr. Herbert Benson runs the Mind/Body Health Institute at Harvard University Medical School. In 1984 he wrote an article in *American Health* (vol. 5, pp. 50–53) called "The Faith Factor." While summarizing the increased use of spiritual techniques such as prayer for helping patients cope with stress and cardiovascular disorders, he cited several research studies of how prayer can produce physiological responses, including decreased heart rate, decreased blood pressure, and a decreased risk of angina episodes in cardiology patients. Later he wrote a book called *Timeless Healing* (New York: Fireside, 1996), in which he described numerous men and women who used prayer as an effective tool for reducing their risk of heart attacks, stress-related illnesses, and strokes.

Prayer and Meditation as a Way of Boosting the Immune System

For centuries spiritual and religious groups have urged their followers to use prayer and meditation as a way to prevent or combat disease. But carefully controlled scientific studies to confirm the benefits of these practices were lacking. This lack began to change, however, in the 1980s, when a substantial amount of careful research was conducted in the emerging field of psychoneuroimmunology (how the mind can influence the immune system to cause or heal illnesses). Respected medical journals began to publish research studies that confirmed what the spiritual and religious groups had been promising—that prayer and meditation can affect our lymphocytes (kinds of white blood cells that produce antibodies to attack infected and cancerous cells, and are responsible for rejecting foreign tissue).

One of the breakthrough studies was published in the *Archives of Internal Medicine* (vol. 145, November 1985, pp. 2110–12). Dr. G. Richard Smith, Jr., and his colleagues at the University of Arkansas College of Medicine in Little Rock used precise laboratory measurements to see if someone trained in spiritual techniques could use those techniques to change her immune system responses. They charted the allergic skin responses and lymphocyte levels of a thirty-nine-year-old woman who at first demonstrated a hypersensitivity to a viral antigen. She was given a skin test weekly for nine weeks. During the first three weeks (phase 1) she was told to react normally, and her body showed a strong allergic response to the antigen. In the second three weeks (phase 2) she was asked to try to inhibit her allergic reaction using any technique she chose. She decided to "visualize higher energies and seek to transform herself into those energies and send healing energy to the injection site." Finally, in phase 3 she was asked to react normally again. She was also asked to repeat the entire sequence nine months later.

The spiritual technique of "connecting with higher energies" helped this woman significantly change not only her skin test results but also the response of her lymphocytes. The researchers concluded that while not every human being has the training or ability to replicate her results, they had been able to show that spiritual visualization and connecting with holy energies can make a crucial impact on the human immune system.

Since 1985 dozens of others studies have replicated these findings and extended them to specific illnesses and conditions. Many of these findings are summarized in the book *Realized Religion: A Bibliographic Essay on the Relationship of Religion and Health,* edited by Theodore Chamberlain and Christopher Hall (Radnor, Pa.: John Templeton Foundation, 2000).

But there is both a hope and a danger in these studies. The hope is that if we become more adept at prayer and meditation, we will be able to affect our immune systems when necessary. The danger is that we will assume doing so is easy or guaranteed, which research shows is not the case. There are many illnesses and conditions that don't respond to spiritual techniques, or that respond only briefly. My concern is that when prayer doesn't seem to have an effect on a physical ailment, men and women shouldn't blame themselves. Nor should they turn away from God or religion when an illness persists or returns. The human body is both miraculous and quite fragile and susceptible. So I urge you to utilize the research on prayer and healing to inspire you to connect with holy energies but not to fall into the trap of expecting or demanding only one kind of result. The universe and our bodies are far more mysterious and complex than that.

Prayer as a Way of Increasing Your Chances of Successful Surgery

In 1991 Theresa Saudia, a registered nurse and captain in the Nurse Corps of the U.S. Air Force, developed a test to find out how helpful prayer was perceived to be for patients dealing with the stress of cardiac surgery. Her study, published in the journal *Heart and Lung* (vol. 20, 1991, pp. 60–65), found that of one hundred people interviewed before, during, and after surgery, 96 percent used prayer as a coping strategy and 70 percent of these rated prayer "extremely helpful" in lessening physiological and psychological stress. What is especially interesting about this study is that the "extremely helpful" rating for prayer came from *both* the people who believed in "internal locus of control" (that they were in charge of their own well-being rather than being determined by external forces) and the people who believed in "external locus of control" (God, luck, doctors, genetics, or other factors beyond an individual's control).

In other words, prayer was deemed "extremely helpful" by people from a variety of belief systems. This study suggests that prayer can have an effect on your physiological and psychological response to surgery whether you believe in God as the still small voice within, God as an all-powerful external universal force, or some combination or variation of these views.

Group Prayer Sessions as a Way of Reducing Painful Symptoms and Enhancing the Patient's Recovery Mechanisms

At Case Western Reserve University Hospital in Cleveland, Drs. Robert Stern, Edward Canda, and Carl Doershuk did a study that explored the controversial question of whether group prayer can help people recover from serious illnesses. Their research focused on families, friends, and congregants praying for loved ones. Men and women from a variety of spiritual backgrounds prayed in large and small groups for each of 402 children, adolescents, and young adults with cystic fibrosis. The findings were reviewed and then published in the *Journal of Adolescent Health* (vol. 13, 1992, pp. 612–15).

Stern and his colleagues found that 92 percent of the patients perceived a benefit from group prayer sessions directed toward their health and recovery. The most common benefits perceived were "a reduction in symptoms," "an ability to maintain their health at a higher level," and "a sense of community and family support." These patients rated group prayer more highly as a treatment aid than chiropractic, nutritional, hypnosis, or acupuncture therapies. Each of these other therapies was beneficial for many of the participants but, according to the patients, to a lesser degree than group prayer. Based on these findings and a host of other cited studies, these researchers recommended that "physician openness and empathy toward patients' beliefs might enhance rapport and facilitate discussion of possible helpful or adverse effects of nonmedical treatments."

The research on group prayer and its effect on the physical healing and emotional well-being of people who have serious illnesses has been explored in several books and articles by Larry Dossey, M.D., of the University of Texas at Dallas. See his books *Healing Words* (New York: Harper-Collins, 1993) and *Reinventing Medicine* (New York: Harper-Collins, 1999).

In addition, during the past few years an extensive study at Duke Clinical Research Institute in Durham, North Carolina, has found strong evidence to support the effectiveness of praying for someone from a distance. In this study 150 patients with recurrent chest pain or heart attacks were randomly assigned to five groups. One of the groups was given standard medical treatments as well as being prayed for from a distance by strangers while the four other groups utilized standard treatments plus healing touch, relaxation therapy, visual imagery, or no additional alternative procedures.

A larger percentage of the patients who were prayed for from a distance had better outcomes than the other four groups. Specifically, those who received standard medical treatment plus "prayer from a distance" had their adverse symptoms reduced by over 50 percent, while the other four groups showed a 30 percent reduction in "adverse outcomes." Does this mean science has proven that praying for someone can make a difference? Some experts say yes while others say no. The Duke study is now being expanded to seven hundred patients and the added factor that some of the patients will know they are being prayed for and some will not. Since these outcomes are still being evaluated, I will reserve comment here. However, you can find this research written up in the *Los Angeles Times,* January 8, 2001, page S5, in an article by Pamela Gerhardt of the *Washington Post.*

Please note that neither these researchers nor I am saying that prayer should be used instead of conventional medicine, or instead of nontraditional treatments such as chiropractic, acupuncture, nutritional changes, and so on. These findings on group prayer and remote prayer simply open up the possibility that heartfelt words and rituals, especially when used in conjunction with other treatment modalities, can have a positive impact in some cases. For many scientists, doctors, and scholars these studies are crucial. But for people of faith the question is usually not whether science proves that prayer can heal someone but rather why not add prayer to the range of treatments for an ailing loved one and see what happens?

Prayer as a Way of Making Marital Relations Better

In 1985 Dr. Leroy Gruner, a professor of sociology at Northern Kentucky University, published "The Correlation of Private Religious Devotional Practices and Marital Adjustment" in the *Journal of Comparative Family Studies* (vol. 16, no. 1, Spring 1985, pp. 47–59). Gruner surveyed 208 couples (416 individuals) and found, "One of the clearest relationships shown by the data was the positive association between prayer as a private religious practice and high marital adjustment," which the study defined as intimacy, affection, confiding in one another, having less frequent disagreements, settling disagreements adequately, and finding happiness in the marriage. He concluded that prayer and other spiritual support mechanisms in these marriages tended to "diminish drastically the minor daily problems and differences between marital partners." The successful marriages still had some disagreements and difficult issues to resolve, but they did so with a stronger sense of harmony and perspective.

There have been numerous other studies correlating prayer and spiritual involvement with marital happiness. Some of these are summarized in a fascinating book called *Religion and Prevention in Mental Health,* edited by Kenneth Pargament (New York: Haworth Press, 1992; see especially p. 67).

Prayer as a Way of Supporting Mental Health and Well-Being

Many researchers have found a correlation between prayer in daily life and several mental health factors. One of the most extensive studies was conducted in 1985 in a random sample survey of 560 residents of Akron, Ohio, by the social researchers Margaret Poloma and Brian Pendleton. Their findings were published in *The Journal of Psychology and Theology* (vol. 19, 1991, pp. 71–83). These statistically valid studies found significant correlations between those who frequently used meditative/contemplative prayer and those who reported feelings of "overall life satisfaction," "existential well-being," "happiness," and "religious satisfaction." It isn't clear whether prayer *causes* the improvements in mental health or simply coincides with it. But their research strongly indicates that in a significant number of individuals there is some relationship between use of meditative prayer and feeling good about life.

In another revealing study, also published in the *Journal of Psychology and Theology* (vol. 16, 1988, pp. 362–68), C. R. Carson, P. E. Bacaseta, and D. A. Simanton ran a test comparing two treatments for psychological distress. One group of college students participated in six sessions of meditative prayer to address their feelings of stress and anxiety. A second group learned a standard psychological technique called progressive relaxation, and a third, the control group, was simply told to relax. The group who had been using meditative prayer "experienced significantly greater reductions in muscle tension, anger, and anxiety" than did students who utilized progressive relaxation or who were in the control group.

Another recent study by M. E. McCullough, published in the *Journal of Counseling Psychology* (vol. 46, 1999, pp. 92–98), also found that spiritual techniques (including prayer) were as effective as and in some cases more effective than standard psychotherapy techniques for reducing or eliminating the symptoms of depression.

I would, however, add the warning that for some individuals who have symptoms of depression, anxiety, emotional volatility, or bursts of anger, prayer alone might not be enough. Some people's psychological symptoms stem from genetic factors, brain chemistry, physiological factors, or other mental health factors that need professional attention and medication, psychotherapy, or a combination of the two to achieve significant improvements.

Yet these studies offer the additional perspective that in some cases there is a spiritual issue underlying anger, depression, or volatility. That's why a growing number of therapists are beginning to explore the use of prayer as well as engaging in counseling conversations about meaning, spiritual values, and connection to one's purpose as part of the healing process. Even if spiritual issues and concerns are only a portion of what causes depression, anxiety, anger, and volatility, addressing these highly personal questions can be beneficial.

Prayer as a Way of Helping Resolve Physical and Emotional Problems

There have also been a few recent studies of how strongly most people seek spiritual assistance when they're going through an emotional or physical problem and the ironic fact that the majority of physicians, psychiatrists, and mental health counselors have neglected to explore or listen openly to their patients' spiritual questions and concerns. For example, a 1981 Gallup poll of Americans from all walks of life found that 95 percent of patients believe in God and 42 percent attend prayer services weekly. Several studies have shown that when people are in emotional or physical distress, they tend to think about God, prayer, and questions of spiritual fate and purpose. But most of the recent research has concluded that a large number of therapists and doctors are neither prepared nor inclined to talk about spiritual questions and issues. For example, in 1988, when the psychologists Scott Richards and Allen Bergin surveyed the entire field of psychotherapists, they found that only 50 percent of therapists considered God or spirituality an important factor in life. (Their research was published in *The Professional Psychologist,* vol. 19, 1988, p. 290). Also, when the American Psychiatric Association surveyed its members a few years later, only 43 percent tended to believe in God, and only 2 percent of psychiatric studies address the spiritual and religious aspects of mental health. (This was reported in *JAMA: The Journal of the American Medical Association* (vol. 273, no. 20, May 1995, p. 1562).

Many times each day in hospitals, clinics, and counseling offices across North America, patients wonder, "Why did God let this happen to me?" and "How do I reconnect on a soul level to improve my chances of healing and recovery?" But if their helping professionals have neither the training nor the interest in assisting them to explore these crucial questions, the patients quickly learn to keep silent with the "experts" about their spiritual concerns.

In very recent years this problem of lack of training has begun to be addressed. In a few nursing journals and some progressive hospitals, studies are going on to help determine whether there is a clear benefit from encouraging a spiritual or religious patient to pray or to discuss spiritual questions with a trained staff member. For many individuals exploring spiritual concerns during a medical or emotional

crisis can become one of the most intimate and healing conversations of a lifetime.

The American Psychological Association has published
two outstanding books to help psychotherapists learn what
they didn't learn in graduate school about how to respond to
their patients' spiritual questions and concerns. *The Hand-
book of Psychology and Religious Diversity,* edited by Scott
Richards and Allen Bergin (Washington, D.C.: APA Books,
2000), addresses the perspectives and needs presented by
counseling clients who come from different spiritual backgrounds, including the diverse issues that tend to be raised
by fundamentalist Christians, liberal Christians, Roman
Catholics, Orthodox Jews, Reform and Conservative Jews,
Buddhists, Muslims, and others. Reading this book as part
of a well-designed training program can help counselors
develop a curiosity about the unique individuals struggling
with issues of faith, guilt, resilience, redemption, and renewal
during a psychological or medical dilemma.

A second book, which includes a wide variety of scientific
studies of the uses and abuses of religion and spirituality in the
counseling process, is *Integrating Spirituality into Treatment,*
edited by William R. Miller (Washington, D.C.: American
Psychological Association, 1999). Each chapter in this book
addresses an aspect of how spirituality can assist counseling
clients, including the proper uses of prayer and meditation,
the effectiveness of spiritual approaches for dealing with
addictive behaviors, the connections between spiritual techniques and cognitive-behavioral techniques, and complex

issues such as surrender, empowerment, hope, forgiveness, acceptance, and serenity. This excellent book can assist any therapist to learn more about how spiritual methods and perspectives can help in cases of depression, anxiety, anger management, addictions, family conflicts, and the search for meaning and purpose.

Finally, in family therapy and social work counseling, there is an outstanding book edited by Froma Walsh of the University of Chicago. Entitled *Spiritual Resources in Family Therapy* (New York: Guilford Press, 1999), it explores the spirituality of resilience, deeper questions involved in recovering from trauma, how to include spiritual issues and conversations in family therapy, and how the therapist can move from an arrogant position of certainty about religious and spiritual issues to a humble position of curiosity about the uniqueness of each individual's spiritual path and perspective.

My hope is for additional resource books and training programs to assist helping professionals do a better job of addressing this important aspect of each person's well-being. Spirituality and health clearly are related—now it's up to the professionals in the health fields to bring our skills and training up-to-date so that we can truly be of service to the people who look to us for guidance and support.

APPENDIX B
Additional Information on Using Prayer for Physical Healing

Here are some additional resources and information to help you or someone you love with prayers for someone who is ill.

Psalms

One of the great Chasidic teachers, Rabbi Nachman of Bratslav, wrote that certain psalms from the Hebrew Bible can assist in healing and renewal during a serious illness. In a recent book by Rabbi Simkha Weintraub of the National Center for Jewish Healing, these psalms are written out and interpreted for use for emotional and physical healing. The psalms are 16, 32, 41, 42, 59, 77, 90, 105, 137, and 150. The book is *Healing of Soul, Healing of Body* (Woodstock, Vt.: Jewish Lights, 1994). It can also be purchased by contacting the National Center for Jewish Healing, 850 Seventh Avenue, Suite 1201, New York, N.Y. 10019, 212-399-2320.

Debbie Perlman, the psalmist in residence at Beth Emet, the Free Synagogue, in Evanston, Illinois, has for years been writing remarkable original psalms for members of her congregation. She recently published a book of these psalms addressing themes that include courage and comfort, centering, surgery, intensive care, healers and caregivers, going home from the hospital, one year later, hospice, diagnosis, yearning, creativity, life changes, personal healing, and renewal. You can order a copy of her 1998 book, *Flames to Heaven: New Psalms for Healing and Praise,* from Rad Publishers, 2849 Birchwood Avenue, Wilmette, Ill. 60091, 847-256-4206.

Prayers

Most prayer books contain several prayers for healing and recovery. In addition, you can order from the National Center for Jewish Healing several guides for personal or group prayers for healing, including *When the Body Hurts, the Soul Still Longs to Sing* (a prayer booklet of heartfelt blessings for times of illness, written by Jewish laywomen); a *Mi Shebeirakh card* (written with full text for men or for women, along with a short explanatory introduction); *A Leader's Guide to Services and Prayers of Healing* (has background on prayer services, suggestions for planning and running a prayer group or service, and sample services); and *Evening and Morning: A Circle of Prayer* (a prayer card with evening and morning prayers for comfort and strength). (National Center for Jewish Healing, 850 Seventh Avenue, Suite 1201, New York, N.Y. 10019, 212-399-2320).

Recently a synagogue in the Los Angeles area, Valley Beth Shalom, printed a guide called *Meditations and Prayers for the Renewal of the Body and Renewal of the Spirit.* It has traditional and personal prayers and reflections on illness and healing that are quite inspiring and helpful. To order a copy (a small voluntary donation is encouraged), you can write Valley Beth Shalom at 15739 Ventura Boulevard, Encino, Calif. 91436-2930 or call 818-995-0526. Their e-mail address is info@vbs.org and their Web site is http://www.vbs.org.

In addition, there is an excellent book of prayers for healing services or personal meditations entitled *Gates of Healing.* Edited by Hirshel Jaffe and H. Leonard Poller and published by Central Conference of American Rabbis (New York, 1988), it is available in both regular and large-print editions.

Finally, in Chapter 5 I described the rendition of the "Mi Shebeirakh" prayer by the singer-songwriter Debbie Friedman. It can be found on several of her cassettes and CDs, including *And You Shall Be a Blessing, Live at the Del, Renewal of Spirit,* and *At Carnegie Hall.* These can be obtained at most Jewish book and music stores or at www.jewishmusic. com and other Internet music sites.

Books on the Ethics, Spirituality, and Practical Steps of Medical Decisions and Treatments

For an extensive guide to Jewish writings on healing and medical ethics from the Bible to current times, I recommend *Illness and Health in the Jewish Tradition,* edited by David Freeman and Judith Abrams (Philadelphia: Jewish Publication Society, 1999). It has rich teachings from a variety of sources and can be found at most Jewish libraries and some Internet bookstores.

Two other helpful and informative books available in Jewish libraries or on the Internet are *Jewish Healing Wisdom* by Steven Rosman (Northvale, N.J.: Jason Aronson, 1997) and *Judaism, Medicine, and Healing* by Ronald Isaacs (Jason Aronson, 1998). These books explore various prayers, ethics, rituals, and scholarly debates concerning how to respond to the illnesses we and our loved ones face.

Counselors and Support Groups

If you would like to find a counselor who can help you or your loved one to locate the right doctors, second opinions, case management, caregiver training, emotional support, and referrals call your nearest Jewish Family Service agency. You can also call the National Association of Jewish Family and Children's Agencies at 1-800-634-7346 and ask for a referral in your area. Or talk with your local rabbi or temple or synagogue administrator to suggest a nearby counselor or agency that can assist you in finding what you need to help improve the chances for healing.

Hospice

The National Center for Jewish Hospice can help you find the right hospice facility and other options for a terminally ill loved one. You can call them at 1-800-446-4448 or ask your local rabbi or Jewish Family Service for information on hospice facilities in your area.

Notes

Introduction

p. 1 *Freud wrote a scathing book* To read more about Freud's views on religion and spirituality, see Sigmund Freud, *The Future of an Illusion* (New York: Norton, 1961), pp. 26–42.

p. 3 *Based on the research of Herbert Benson* See Herbert Benson, *Timeless Healing: The Power and Biology of Belief* (New York: Fireside, 1997).

p. 3 *Joan Borysenko* See Joan Borysenko, *Fire in the Soul: A New Psychology of Spiritual Optimism* (New York: Warner, 1994).

p. 3 *Larry Dossey* See Larry Dossey, *Healing Words: The Power of Prayer and the Practice of Medicine* (New York: Harper, 1997).

p. 3 *Jon Kabat-Zinn* See Jon Kabat-Zinn, *Full Catastrophe Living: Using the Wisdom of the Body and Mind to Free Stress, Pain and Illness* (New York: Delta, 1990).

p. 3 *Bernie Siegel* See Bernie Siegel, *Love, Medicine and Miracles* (New York: Warner, 1990).

p. 8 *Millions of non-Jews are reading* See Thomas Cahill, *The Gifts of the Jews* (New York: Anchor, 1999); Harold Kushner, *How Good Do We Have to Be* (Boston: Little, Brown, 1997); Naomi Levy, *To*

Begin Again (New York: Ballantine, 1999); David Wolpe, *Making Loss Matter* (New York: Riverhead, 1999); and Yitta Halberstam and Judith Leventhal, *Small Miracles* (Holbrook, Massachusetts: Adams Media, 1997).

p. 13 *"The still small voice within"* In the Bible 1 Kings 19:12, Elijah the prophet says "and Adonai was not in the fire but in a still small voice."

p. 13 *Jewish concept of the Shekhinah* For more on this Jewish sense of the in-dwelling Presence of God, see Lynn Gottlieb, *She Who Dwells Within* (San Francisco: Harper, 1995) and Cecil Roth, ed., *Encyclopedia Judaica* (Philadelphia: Coronet, 1994), s.v. "Shechinah."

1. A Prayer to Help You Start Each Morning with a Much Better Frame of Mind

p. 17 *My life has been a tapestry of rich and royal hue* Lyric from "Tapestry," words and music by Carole King. Copyright © 1971, 1999 Colgems-EMI Music, Inc., New York, New York. Used with permission.

p. 19 *The phrase "Modeh Ani" first appeared* This comes from the Talmud, Berachot 60b.

p. 20 *Shortened twelve-word "Modeh ani"* Macy Nulman, *The Encyclopedia of Jewish Prayer* (Northvale, New Jersey: Jason Aronson, 1996), p. 251.

p. 20 *According to Reuven Hammer* Reuven Hammer, *Entering Jewish Prayer* (New York: Schocken, 1994), p. 24.

p. 22 *Bluma Zeigarnik was studying human perception* For more information on the Zeigarnik effect, see David Sills, ed., *The International Encyclopedia of the Social Sciences,* vol. 5 (New York: Macmillan, 1968), p. 407, or the original *Das Behalten erledigter und underledigter Handlungen. Untersuchungen zur Handlungs und Affektspsychologie,* No. 3 *Psychologische forschung* 9: 1927, pp. 1–85.

p. 24 *In the writings of the Kabbalah* For more on the Jewish mystical sense of the soul, see Simcha Paull Raphael, *Jewish Views of the Afterlife* (Northvale, New Jersey: Jason Aronson, 1996), pp. 278–79; Gershom Scholem, *Kabbalah* (New York: New American Library, 1978), p. 155; or Isaiah Tishby and Fischel Lachower, *The Wisdom of the Zohar,* vol. 2, trans. David Goldstein (London: Oxford University Press, 1989), pp. 684–85.

p. 27 *Rabbi Isaac Luria* For more on Luria's views of soul, hidden sparks, and purpose, see Rifat Sonsino and Daniel Syme, *Finding God: Ten Jewish Responses* (New York: Union of American Hebrew Congregations, 1986), pp. 67–77, and David Cooper, *God Is a Verb* (New York: Riverhead, 1997), pp. 28–29, 108, 181–82.

p. 32 *Discussed in detail in Harold Kushner's book* Harold Kushner, *When Bad Things Happen to Good People* (New York: Schocken, 1981).

p. 33 *If an innocent child dies* For different Jewish mystical and traditional theories on suffering by innocents, see Shmuel Boteach, *Wrestling with the Divine* (Northvale, New Jersey: Jason Aronson, 1995), pp. 155, 181, 218.

p. 34 *Elie Wiesel* For more on Wiesel's theological views, see Elie Wiesel, *All Rivers Run to the Sea* (New York: Schocken, 1996);

Ibid., *The Sea Is Never Full* (New York: Knopf, 1999); and Ibid., *The Trial of God* (New York: Random House, 1995).

p. 34 *Wiesel recently wrote a Yom Kippur statement* This statement, entitled "A Prayer for the Days of Awe," was written by Elie Wiesel and published in the *Los Angeles Jewish Times* vol.102, no. 31 (September 1999). Used by permission.

p. 39 *Rabbi Yose advised* See Reuven Hammer, *Entering Jewish Prayer* (New York: Schocken, 1994), p. 293, and the Talmud, Y. Berachot 8:1.

p. 39 *Rabbi Aryeh Kaplan suggests* See Aryeh Kaplan, *Jewish Meditation: A Practical Guide* (New York: Schocken, 1985), pp. 93–94.

2. A Prayer to Help You Refocus When You're Feeling Stressed or Distracted

p. 49 *A scholar named Rabbi Samson ben Zodok* See Tashbaz 276, Shulchan Aruch OH 4:18 or *Encyclopedia Judaica,* vol. 12 (Jerusalem: Keter Publishing, 1972), pp. 998–99.

p. 52 *Kitzur Shulchan Aruch . . . written in 1870 by Rabbi Solomon Ganzfried* For a modern translation, see Rabbi Avrohom Davis, trans., *The Metsudah Kitzur Shulchan Aruch* (Brooklyn, New York: Metsudah Publications, 1987).

p. 59 *Doubt and disbelief* Rabbi Zalman Schachter-Shalomi's way of looking at doubt and degrees of belief was presented at the 1993 Davenology Workshops in Los Angeles and in 1995 in Fort Collins, Colorado. It was also quoted by Rabbi Jonathan Omer-man in Rodger Kamenetz, *Stalking Elijah* (New York: Harper, 1997), p. 77.

3. A Prayer to Resolve Tension and Misunderstandings Between You and Someone Else

p. 72 *"Fight-or-flight"* See Philip Zimbardo, *Psychology and Life* (Glenview, Illinois: Scott, Foresman and Company, 1985), p. 499.

p. 76 *The nineteenth-century scholar named Naphtali Zevi Judah Berlin* See Ha'amek Davar's commentaries on the Torah, published in 1879–80 and discussed in Nehama Leibowitz, *Studies in Bamidbar [Numbers]* (Jerusalem: World Zionist Organization Ahva Press, 1980), pp. 65–67.

p. 78 *Rabbi Ovadiah of Sforno, Italy* See Rabbi Nosson Scherman, ed., *The Stone Edition Chumash* (Brooklyn, New York: Artscroll Mesorah Publications, 1993), pp. 762–63.

p. 79 *Moreinu HaRav Zeev Wolf Einhorn* Ibid., p. 763.

p. 84 *Microsoft* Encarta Dictionary Microsoft *Encarta Dictionary* (New York: St. Martin's Press, 1999).

p. 84 *Rebuke in most Jewish sources* See *Encyclopedia Judaica,* vol. 13 (Jerusalem: Keter Publishing, 1972), p. 1606.

p. 84 *According to Moses ben Maimon* See Yad, De'ot 6:6,7 or *Encyclopedia Judaica,* vol. 13 (Jerusalem: Keter Publishing, 1972).

p. 85 *Rabbi Nathan said* See the Babylonian Talmud, Bava Metzia 59b, or H. N. Bialik and Y. H. Ravnitzky, eds., *The Book of Legends* (New York: Schocken, 1992), pp. 693–96.

p. 85 *Rabbi Akiva remarked* See the Babylonian Talmud, Arakhin 16b or *Encyclopedia Judaica,* vol. 13 (Jerusalem: Keter Publishing, 1972).

4. A Prayer So You Can Unwind and
Find Peace at Least Three Times a Day

p. 96 *Saying a blessing before eating goes back thousands of years* See *Encyclopedia Judaica*, vol. 7: (Jerusalem: Keter Publishing, 1972), p. 841.

p. 96 *The Israelites waited for food to be blessed* In the Bible, 1 Sam. 9:13 says "As soon as you are come into the city, you shall straightway find the seer, before he goes up to the high place to eat; for the people will not eat until he comes, because he blesses the sacrifice; and afterwards they eat that are bidden."

p. 96 *Flavius Josephus described in detail* See Josephus, *Wars*, vol. 2 (Grand Rapids, Michigan: Kregel, 1999), p. 131, which is summarized in *Encyclopedia Judaica*, vol. 7: (Jerusalem: Keter Publishing, 1972), p. 841.

p. 98 *The prayer before eating is not just for offering thanks* See Evelyn Garfiel, *Service of the Heart: A Guide to the Jewish Prayer Book* (Northvale, New Jersey: Jason Aronson, 1989), pp. 201–2.

p. 102 *Bread is considered the "staff of life"* In Orah Hayyim 204: 12, a section of the 'Arba'ah Turim and the Shulchan Arukh, Joseph Caro writes "When one eats several foods that have different blessings, the more significant food determines the benediction to be recited."

p. 102 *Consider the specific source of nourishment* The different prayers for different types of foods are found in *The Complete Artscroll Siddur* (Brooklyn, New York: Artscroll Mesorah Publications, 1994), pp. 224–25.

p. 105 *God as an active force* See David Cooper, *God Is a Verb* (New York: Riverhead, 1997), pp. 65–66.

p. 105 *In the Jewish mystical tradition* This active force is described in the book *Pri Eytz Hadar (Fruit of the Beautiful Tree)* by the followers of Isaac Luria and summarized in Arthur Waskow, *Down-to-Earth Judaism* (New York: William Morrow, 1995), pp. 101–3.

p. 106 *"For centuries Jewish mystics"* From Marcia Prager, *The Path of Blessing* (New York: Bell Tower, 1998), pp. 20–22. Used with permission.

p. 107 *Luria and his followers described how a two-way process happens* This is summarized in *Pri Eytz Hadar (Fruit of the Beautiful Tree);* Arthur Waskow, *Down-to-Earth Judaism* (New York: William Morrow, 1995); Marcia Prager, *The Path of Blessing* (New York: Bell Tower, 1998); and Daniel Matt, *The Essential Kabbalah* (New York: Harper, 1994), pp. 148–53.

p. 108 *Prayer over food can draw down* shefa See Aryeh Kaplan, *Meditation and Kabbalah* (York Beach, Maine: Samuel Weiser, 1982), p. 227.

p. 109 *Paraphrasing from several Chasidic masters* Matt cites Isaac Luria (sixteenth century) and Levi Yitzhak of Berditchev (eighteenth century) as the sources for this description. See Daniel Matt, *The Essential Kabbalah* (New York: Harper, 1994).

5. A Prayer to Help Heal the Body and
the Soul of You or Someone You Love

p. 117 *The current research findings of psychoneuroimmunology*
For a brief summary, see Appendix A.

p. 119 *According to Macy Nulman* See Macy Nulman, *The Encyclopedia of Jewish Prayer* (Northvale, New Jersey: Jason Aronson, 1993), p. 244.

p. 119 *The tradition says* See *Encyclopedia Judaica*, vol. 12 (Jerusalem: Keter Publishing, 1972), pp. 86–87.

p. 123 *The keys to health and well-being* See Bernie Siegel, *Love, Medicine and Miracles* (New York: Warner, 1990) and Philip Zimbardo, *Psychology and Life* (Glenview, Illinois: Scott, Foresman and Company, 1985) s.v. "Health Psychology," pp. 490–96.

p. 124 *When we pray for healing* See Abraham Twersky, *Living Each Day* (Brooklyn, New York: Mesorah Publications, 1988).

p. 125 *1985 Ph.D. dissertation* Michael I. Brown, *I Am Lord Your Healer: A Philological Study of the Root Rapa in the Hebrew Bible and the Ancient Near East* (New York: New York University, 1985). A copy of this dissertation on the definitive translation of *refu-ah sh'leimah* can be found on microfiche 86-04041 at the Ostrow Library at the University of Judaism in Los Angeles.

p. 129 *God's role in our illnesses* See Nancy Flam, "Reflections Toward a Theology of Illness and Healing," *Sh'ma* (May 27, 1994), pp. 1–4. Used with permission from both the journal editor, Susan Berrin, and the author, Nancy Flam. Thanks to Ellen Winer, R.N., for recommending it.

p. 129 *The din that Moses Cordovera . . . talks about* See Moses Cordovera, *Pardes Rimonim,* chapter 8.

p. 132 *The world was created for the sake of a single individual* See Mishna Sanhedrin 4:5. It is explored in Joseph Telushkin, *Jewish Wisdom* (New York: Morrow, 1994), pp. 88–90.

p. 133 *The major exception on Sabbath* See Macy Nulman, *The Encyclopedia of Jewish Prayer* (Northvale, New Jersey: Jason Aronson, 1996), p. 244.

p. 135 *A well-established tradition of giving charity soon after saying the "Mi shebeirakh"* See *The Complete Artscroll Siddur* (Brooklyn, New York: Artscroll Mesorah Publications, 1994), pp. 443–44; the Babylonian Talmud Beitzah 366; and Macy Nulman, *The Encyclopedia of Jewish Prayer* (Northvale, New Jersey: Jason Aronson, 1996), p. 244.

p. 135 *Creates merit for that individual* See *Encyclopedia Judaica,* vol. 12 (Philadelphia: Coronet, 1994), pp. 86–89.

p. 135 *All our souls are connected in the great womb of life* This interpretation was described in a course titled "Healing the Body, Healing the Soul" by Rabbi Amy Eilberg, *Aleph* Kallah, Fort Collins, Colorado, July 1995; in Ps. 36:8; and in Lynn Gottlieb, *She Who Dwells Within* (San Francisco: Harper, 1995).

p. 136 *According to the mystical tradition in Judaism* This was discussed at the Metivta Healing Conference, Los Angeles, 1999. It is also discussed in Num. 15:7 as "Do not harden your heart nor shut your hand," and in various spiritual terms in Solomon Ganzfried, *The Metsudah Kitzur Shulchan Aruch.* Modern translation:

Rabbi Avrohom Davis, trans., *The Metsudah Kitzur Shulchan Aruch* (Brooklyn, New York: Metsudah Publications, 1987), pp. 358–59.

p. 141   *Rabbi Aryeh Hirschfield . . . has written a beautiful melody* Used with permission.

6. A Prayer for Breaking Free from a Habit That Hurts You or Others

p. 149   *One of the most beautiful teachings of Jewish spirituality* This comes from the Babylonian Talmud, Berakhot 34b, and is described in Joseph Telushkin, *Jewish Wisdom* (New York: William Morrow, 1994), p. 348.

p. 151   *The Mussar movement* For more on this approach to spiritual self-improvement and conquering bad habits, see *Encyclopedia Judaica*, vol. 12 (Philadelphia: Coronet, 1994), s.v. "Musar Movement," pp. 534–35; Zalman Ury, *The Musar Movement* (New York: Yeshiva University Press, 1969); or Stuart Linke, *Psychological Perspectives on Traditional Jewish Practices* (Northvale, New Jersey: Jason Aronson, 1999), s.v. Musar and Israel Salanter, pp. 22–31.

p. 152   *Personal growth themes inherent in each of these traditions* For more on how to seek out the deeper meanings and personal improvement opportunities from Jewish holidays, see Arthur Waskow, *Seasons of Our Joy* (New York: Bantam, 1982) and Irving Greenberg, *The Jewish Way: Living the Holidays* (New York: Simon and Schuster, 1988).

p. 155   *A shivviti was utilized in many traditional congregations* See *Encyclopedia Judaica*, vol. 14 (Philadelphia: Coronet, 1994), p. 1419.

p. 155 *Spiritual retreat with . . . Rabbi Ted Falcon of Seattle* A February 1995 Friends of Bet Alef workshop conducted in Los Angeles.

p. 157 *The Baal Shem Tov . . . two-step remedy* This is based on the Talmudic suggestion in TB Abodah Zarah 20a and is discussed in Rodger Kamenetz, *The Jew in The Lotus* (New York: Harper, 1994), p. 126.

p. 158 *Teshuvah and personal renewal in Jewish spirituality* For more on how to turn in a more holy direction, see Leonard Kravitz and Kerry Olitzky, *The Journey of the Soul: Traditional Sources on Teshuvah* (Northvale, New Jersey: Jason Aronson, 1995).

7. A Prayer to Help You End the Day with Deeper Insights and Serenity

p. 173 *More than 60 percent of adults have trouble falling asleep* See "Can't Sleep?" *Los Angeles Times* (February 22, 2000), Living Section, p. 1.

p. 175 *Declaration of belief in one unifying God* See Lawrence Hoffman, *My People's Prayer Book*, vol. 1: *The Sh'ma and Its Blessings* (Woodstock, Vermont: Jewish Lights, 1997), pp. 87–91; and *Shema Yisrael*, trans. and commentary by Rabbi Meir Zlotowitz (Brooklyn, New York: Mesorah Publications, 1982), p. 15.

p. 176 *According to Yitzhak Buxbaum* See Yitzhak Buxbaum, *Jewish Spiritual Practices* (Northvale, New Jersey: Jason Aronson, 1990), p. 542.

p. 177 *The complete Hebrew prayer* See *The Complete Artscroll Siddur* (Brooklyn, New York: Artscroll Mesorah Publications, 1994).

p. 180   *In Judaism, forgiveness is a duty* See *Encyclopedia Judaica* vol. 6 (Philadelphia: Coronet, 1994), p. 1437.

p. 180   *The Talmud says, "The quality of forgiveness"* See Yer. 79a, Num R. 8:4, Yad, Teshuvah 2:10.

p. 180   *Forgiveness in the Kabbalistic tradition* See David Cooper, *God Is a Verb* (New York: Riverhead, 1997), p. 244.

p. 181   *The Hebrew word for forgiveness,* mokheil See Ernest Klein, *A Comprehensive Etymological Dictionary of the Hebrew Language* (New York: Macmillan, 1987).

p. 181   *The Talmud says that a person who has been wronged should be pliant as a reed* Ta'an, 20a.

p. 181   *Forgive so that your own heart won't become hardened* As described by Rabbi Mordecai Finley, Congregation Ohr HaTorah, April 1996.

p. 182   *You write down briefly* See Yitzhak Buxbaum, *Jewish Spiritual Practices* (Northvale, New Jersey: Jason Aronson, 1990), pp. 540–47.

p. 185   *The guidelines of Maimonides* These are described in Hilchos Tefillah 7:1 and explained in *The Complete Artscroll Siddur* (Brooklyn, New York: Artscroll Mesorah Publications, 1994), p. 288.

p. 186   *Asking God to help you answer a specific question during your dreams* See Tamar Frankiel and Judy Greenfield, *Entering the Temple of Dreams* (Woodstock, Vermont: Jewish Lights, 2000), pp. 130–42; and Stuart Linke, *Psychological Perspectives on Traditional Jewish Practices* (Northvale, New Jersey: Jason Aronson, 1999), pp. 211–14.

p. 193   *A promise you make to yourself* See Rabbi Meir Zlotowitz, *Shema Yisrael*, trans. and commentary by Rabbi Meir Zlotowitz (Brooklyn, New York: Mesorah Publications, 1982), p. 205; and Lawrence Hoffman, *My People's Prayer Book*, vol. 1: *The Sh'ma and Its Blessings* (Woodstock, Vermont: Jewish Lights, 1997), pp. 100–104.

p. 193   *Rabbi Debra Orenstein . . . offered a beautiful interpretation* At UCLA Ackerman Union, Makom Ohr Shalom services, September 2000.

About the Author

Leonard Felder, Ph.D., is a licensed psychologist in private practice in West Los Angeles and the author of eight books, including *The Ten Challenges, A Fresh Start, Making Peace with Yourself, When a Loved One Is Ill,* and the best-seller *Making Peace with Your Parents,* coauthored with Harold Bloomfield, which was named Nonfiction Book of the Year by *Medical Self-Care Magazine.* Dr. Felder's books have sold over 950,000 copies and been translated into thirteen languages.

A frequently requested speaker on spirituality and psychology, Dr. Felder has given guest sermons, workshops, and courses at more than forty temples and synagogues throughout the United States. He has given over 180 radio and television interviews, including with Oprah Winfrey, Sally Jessy Raphael, and The Early Show with Bryant Gumbel, and on NBC News, CNN, and A.M. Canada. He was recently keynote speaker at the California Association of Marriage and Family Therapists Annual Conference on how to utilize spirituality in the healing process.

Dr. Felder's articles on Jewish spirituality and personal growth have been published in dozens of magazines and newspapers, including fourteen Jewish newspapers nationwide, in *Reform Judaism Magazine,* and in mainstream magazines such as *New Woman, Redbook, Family Circle, Men's Health, Glamour,* and *American Health.*

Active in several volunteer organizations, Dr. Felder received the Distinguished Merit Citation of the National Conference of Christians and Jews for developing adult and teen workshops on overcoming racism, sexism, homophobia, and religious prejudice. He also cofacilitated the first ongoing dialogue series between Jews and Germans whose parents lived during the Holocaust.

He and his wife, Linda Schorin, live in Mar Vista, California, with their son, Steven.